Truth Wars

Truth Wars

Talking About Tolerance

Edited by Tony Watkins

Copyright © 2005 The Damaris Trust

First published in 2005 by Damaris Books, an imprint of Authentic Media, 9 Holdom Avenue, Bletchley, Milton Keynes, MK1 1QR, UK and 129 Mobilization Drive, Waynesboro, GA 30830-4575, USA

The right of the authors to be identified as the authors of this work has been asserted by them in accordance with the Copyright, Designs and Patents Act 1988.

All rights reserved. No part of this publication may be reproduced or transmitted in any form or by any means, electronic or mechanical, including photocopy, recording or any information storage and retrieval system, without permission in writing from the publisher.

British Library Cataloguing in Publication Data

A catalogue record for this book is available from the British Library

1-904753-12-4

Unless otherwise indicated, all Scripture quotations are taken from the *Holy Bible*, New Living Translation, copyright © 1996. Used by permission of Tyndale House Publishers, Inc., Wheaton, Illinois 60189, USA. All rights reserved.

Cover design by fourninezero design
Typeset by GCS, Leighton Buzzard, Beds,
in 11 on 13 Palatino
Print management by Adare Carwin
Printed in the UK by Haynes, Sparkford, Yeovil, Somerset

Contents

Introduction to the *Talking About* Series by Tony Watkins		vii
Acknowledgements		xi
Introduction by Nick Pollard		xiii
1.	Ministry of Dissent by Nick Pollard	1
2.	All Inclusive – A Biblical Perspective on Tolerance by Tony Watkins	15
3.	Testing Tolerance by Tony Watkins	33
4.	Lip Service by Louise Crook	49

5.	*Saved!* – Study Guide by Louise Crook	57
6.	*Hero* – Study Guide by Louise Griffiths	69
7.	*Not the End of the World* – Study Guide by Tony Watkins	79
8.	*Doctor Who* – Study Guide by Tony Watkins	91
9.	Definitely Maybe – the Philosophy of David Hume by Peter S. Williams	103

Background to the Featured Quotes   119

Further Reading   129

Introduction to the *Talking About* Series

Have you ever had one of those conversations when you know you ought to be able to bring in a Christian perspective? The problem is how to do it. As the conversation goes on you become more and more anxious. You know you have a good opportunity to say something; you know you *should* say something – but you just can't think what. Probably all of us have been there at some time or other. Many of us would like a little help on thinking through some issues beforehand.

It seems to me that there are three areas of conversation which frequently cry out for a Christian angle to be included: personal issues in the lives of friends, family or work colleagues; big issues in society generally; and things in the media. They often overlap, of course. So when Nick Pollard was asked to contribute a regular column for *Idea*, the Evangelical Alliance's magazine for members,[1] it seemed a great opportunity to focus on some of the overlapping issues which people are talking about. The articles aim to help readers understand some of what is being said about these issues in today's world, and particularly to explore some of the underlying ideas. The primary aim, of course, is to help equip people for having more and more productive conversations with friends, colleagues and family. It soon became apparent that this is just the kind of help that many Christians feel they need.

So, this series of short books came to be. Each of the books takes the basic ingredients of what Nick has written in one of his articles and develops them into something more substantial, but still light and easily digested. Nick significantly develops his 800-word *Idea* article into the opening chapter of each book. Then come some extra ingredients: a biblical perspective on the issue; articles on key aspects of the central theme; study guides on relevant films, books or television programmes (note: these may contain plot spoilers); and an introduction to one or more key thinkers whose work still influences our culture. Some of these chapters have been developed from material published on Damaris' CultureWatch website (www.culturewatch. org), others have been commissioned especially for this book. Finally, sprinkled throughout the mix are some great quotes which help to spice up your conversations about the issues we're examining (many of these quotes have come from another great Damaris resource, www. ToolsForTalks.com – a collection of tools for speakers whether they are teaching the Bible to Christians or engaged in evangelism).

This is not the kind of book to sit down and read straight through. Instead it has been designed for dipping into. Each of the chapters stands independently of the others, though of course they're all linked by the common theme. One of the consequences of this is that you will, at times, find a little overlap between chapters. We've minimised this as much as we can without taking away anything essential from one or

Introduction to the Talking About *Series*

more of the chapters. The study guides are suitable for individual reflection or for use in home groups. If you do use them in a group setting, don't slavishly work through all the questions – we've given you more than enough so that you can select some that you feel are particularly helpful to your group. Finally, the last chapter, introducing an influential thinker, is inevitably harder going than earlier chapters – which is why it is at the end of the book. It is worth taking time to try to understand the line of argument and why it is significant, but the chapter is not essential for getting to grips with the central issue around which the book revolves.

We hope you will find this interesting, entertaining and stimulating. But our prayer is that this will enable you to be more effective in talking about the good news of Jesus Christ within today's world, whether – as Nick frequently says – you are talking from a pulpit or over the garden fence.

Tony Watkins

Note

[1] For more information, contact Evangelical Alliance at 186 Kennington Park Road, London, SE11 4BT or visit their website: www.eauk.org

Acknowledgements

I am extremely grateful to all the writers who have contributed to this book, and to the series as a whole. It is a joy to work with people who are so committed to thoroughly analysing facets of our culture in order to help Christians in their discipleship and evangelism, and to help those who are not yet Christians begin to see the extraordinary relevance of the Christian faith.

Particular thanks go to Nick Pollard whose insightful writing is the foundation for the books, and who provides many helpful suggestions on material for inclusion. Thanks also to Steve Couch, Managing Editor of Damaris Books, for his constant support and input during the many stages of pulling the books together, and to the team at Authentic Media who handle the production of the books and with whom we enjoy a strong partnership.

Introduction

'Why can't you just accept that different people have different beliefs, and that they are all equally true. Why are you so intolerant?'

The student who said this to me had taken offence that I had raised certain ethical questions about homosexual activity. I had just spent the previous hour helping this student, and a group of others, to explore the scientific data concerning homosexuality. We had looked at a wide range of published research into the incidence and nature of homosexual activity, as well as the attempts to identify a genetic (or other biological) basis for homosexual inclination.

As we did this, it became clear that they were uncomfortable with this data – not because they had reasons to doubt its accuracy, but because it seemed to conflict with their assumptions. And so I gently raised ethical questions about whether homosexual activity could be considered 'good'. They asked me what I believed, and I explained that the data drove me to the conclusion that homosexual sex is not really 'good sex'.

This immediately provoked the accusation of intolerance. The students made it clear that this was not a view they would tolerate. Strangely, they didn't see the irony of accusing me of intolerance whilst not tolerating my view.

As the conversation progressed, they asked me if I would accept that other people have different views from mine, and that – if we are tolerant – we must accept these different views as equally true. I tried to help them to separate those two questions. The first one is straightforward. Certainly other people do hold different views. We live in a society full of different views – it is a plural society. The second is more difficult. Does tolerance mean that we must always accept different views as equally true? Or, put another way, does the *sociological* fact of a plural society necessarily entail a *philosophical* acceptance of pluralism?

This is a very important question, especially for those of us who are Christians. We believe in the absolute truth claims of Jesus. But we live in a world in which most people do not. We want to communicate the Christian gospel appropriately in this world. But we find that many of our conversations about spiritual and moral issues in general, and about Christian faith in particular, turn into conversations (and sometimes, sadly, arguments) about the nature of truth and tolerance.

So, if our conversations are going to help people, then we must give adequate thought to the concept of truth, and what it means to be tolerant. That is what this book is designed to help you to do.

Nick Pollard

If our goal is to achieve a multicultural society that is both free and peaceful, then what we need is not the multiplication of taboos but the expansion of tolerance. The belief in the value of tolerance is not like a belief in Jesus Christ, the prophet Muhammad, Ahura Mazda or, for that matter, the scientific wisdom of Darwin; it's the belief that alone makes it possible for all other beliefs to coexist.

Timothy Garton Ash

1. Ministry of Dissent

Nick Pollard

I was recently a guest lecturer at a media college, teaching ethical philosophy to a group of trainee journalists. I asked them what they thought was the most fundamental basis for ethics. Their almost universal reply was a single word: *tolerance*.

Many have observed that tolerance seems to have become the touchstone of morality in our culture. Tolerance seems to be the ultimate virtue. And an accusation of intolerance seems to be the most damning criticism that anyone can face.

These students told me that we should be tolerant of everyone and everything. I tried to help them to think more deeply about this by demonstrating that they did not really believe what they were saying. 'Imagine,' I said, 'that someone has been picking his nose all the way through my lecture. But I am a very tolerant person and so I have not objected to this. I have just let him get on with it; if that is what he wants to do, then I will let him do it.' From their murmurs of approval, it was clear that they considered this was a good thing. My tolerance was a virtue. 'And now imagine,' I continued, 'that a few minutes ago a man came in at the back of the lecture theatre with a carving knife, and he has been working his way along the back row, stabbing people to death. Now, would it be good for me to tolerate him? Should I just let him get on with doing what he wants to do?' It was clear that they did not think that this type of tolerance was good. 'So,' I suggested, 'we do seem to believe that there are certain things that should not be tolerated. If so, this raises questions: How do we decide what to tolerate and what not to tolerate? If we don't think that tolerance means "tolerating anything and everything", what do we really mean by the word?'

Talking About Tolerance

The questions I explored with these students are raised quite often in our culture. They are usually stimulated by particular events in the news, or particular films in the cinemas. Let's look at a few recent examples.

In October 2004, many people began talking about Rocco Buttiglione, Italy's choice as the European Union's Commissioner for Justice, Freedom and Security. Mr Buttiglione is a philosopher as well as a politician, 'a man equally at home giving an ethics seminar as discussing practical solutions to Europe's immigration issues.'[1] A 56-year-old father of four, he is a Christian Democrat and had been Italy's European Affairs minister since 2001. He is also a devoted Roman Catholic, and that was where the problem arose. MEPs questioned Mr Buttiglione for three hours about his views on some of the issues which come under his new portfolio (including immigration and security). Some of his responses raised concerns, but it was his remarks on homosexuality that sparked such outrage that he was forced to withdraw his candidacy.

He dared to express his view that homosexual behaviour is a sin. He was very careful to make it clear that this did not mean that he thought it should be criminalized. He said:

> 'I may think that homosexuality is a sin, and this has no effect on politics, unless I say that homosexuality is a crime.'[2]

However, a whole host of MEPs demanded that he be stripped of his portfolio – and so he withdrew.

The controversy generated a great deal of discussion in the media, and in pubs and offices. A lot of that discussion centred around the nature of religious views. In a liberal democracy, how do we handle the fact that some people hold religious views that are contrary to popular opinion? In particular, if people hold a position of authority, is it contrary to the principles of a liberal democracy if they also hold such religious beliefs? Or is this actually the fundamental basis of liberal democracy?

Meanwhile, in the cinemas, a particular film was also sparking a similar debate, but from a personal rather than political perspective. *Saved!* (MGM, 2004) is a controversial film which tells the story of Mary and her final year at a Christian high school. Mary discovers that her boyfriend Dean thinks he is gay and so she tries to cure him – by seducing him into having sex with her. She doesn't cure him, but she does become pregnant. Her Christian friends ostracize her, and she turns instead to a disabled boy and a Jewish girl, who are both already quite familiar with this experience.[3]

The film's website says that, 'the film speaks out against those who are intolerant and their inability to open their hearts and minds to others' way of thinking.'[4] They claim that they are not criticising Christians specifically, but the fact that the story is set in a Christian community makes this inevitable. As a result, the film tends to reinforce the view that there is something inherently intolerant about Christian faith – and that this is not acceptable. If Rocco Buttiglione had to change his job because he was accused of intolerance, should Christians also change their faith if they are accused of intolerance?

Then, hot on the heels of these two controversies, around Christmas 2004, three events hit the headlines and caused almost everyone (even those who had missed the debate concerning Buttiglione and *Saved!)* to talk about tolerance. First, the Birmingham Repertory Theatre staged a play called *Behzti* which told the story of sexual abuse and rape in a Sikh temple. A few weeks later, the BBC held a Jerry Springer Night in which they showed *Jerry Springer – The Opera*. Packed with obscenities, this performance represented Jesus as a nappy-wearing fetishist. Then a few days later, the front pages of UK newspapers were covered with photographs of Prince Harry wearing a Nazi uniform, complete with a swastika armband, at a fancy dress party. This was particularly offensive because of the timing – just a few weeks before the sixtieth anniversary of the liberation of Auschwitz.

All of these events created outrage amongst different groups. In particular, Sikhs protested about *Behzti*, Christians protested about *Jerry Springer – The Opera*, and Jews protested about Prince Harry's Nazi uniform. Consequently, *Behzti* was cancelled and Prince Harry apologized. But the BBC refused to cancel or apologise for *Jerry Springer – The Opera*. Indeed, much of the discussion around this subject centred instead upon accusations that Christians are – once again – being intolerant, illustrated by the National Secular Society's accusation that Christians were being 'religious bullies'.[5]

Clearly then, if Christians are to engage in reasonable discussion on such issues we must be able to help people to understand what tolerance is – and, in this contemporary culture, it will not be easy. But it must begin with us understanding the meaning and nature of tolerance for ourselves – and perhaps this should begin with a consideration of the meaning and nature of beliefs about truth.

Talking About Truth

When people express a belief, or a truth claim, what do they mean? Let's look at two philosophical approaches to this question, and see how this impacts upon the question of tolerance.

There is a philosophical approach which argues that different beliefs are actually only the result of different people looking at the same thing from different perspectives.

The classic story that is usually told to illustrate this is that of an elephant that is taken into a room full of blind people who have to guess what it is. They all get different perspectives because the elephant is so big that they can only touch different parts of it. One feels the tail, one feels the trunk, one feels a leg, and so on. Thus, they all come up with different suggestions about what the thing is because they all perceive it differently. Similarly, it is argued, truth about any issue in life is always so big that we can only have a very limited perspective on it, and so we must be tolerant of others who see it differently.

More recently, this was illustrated in the film *Hero* (Miramax, 2004). This told the story of a Chinese king and a group of assassins. But the story wasn't just told once, it was re-told and re-told. Each time some key facts remained the same, but other 'facts' changed, and the interpretation of the sequence of events was very different. Each scene was filmed almost entirely in different colours and these, according to Jet Li (who played Nameless in the film), 'talk about the different story perspectives'.[6]

As with any philosophical approach, one can trace its roots in the thinking of past philosophers, and its shoots in today's world.

For example, this approach has roots in the work of the empiricist philosopher David Hume (1711–1776). Hume believed that all knowledge of reality comes from the five senses which make impressions upon us, and which form the basis of ideas in our mind. Thus human knowledge becomes an interpretation of human experience. So, according to this idea, we must be sceptical about our understanding of the real world since it depends upon the way in which we interpret it. Your interpretation may be different from mine. Then, this approach clearly affects many postmodern thinkers. Postmodern historians, for example, will not talk about history in terms of any objective reality that can be established. Rather they argue that we all have our own views of history which come from our own perspectives on the world. Thus they will talk of 'feminist history' or 'black history' or 'gay history' ('queer history' as it's now known) – history as told through the perspectives of different people.

There is another philosophical approach which focuses not just on different perspectives of different people, but on different perspectives within the same person according to the roles that we play in different phases of our lives. One story that is told to illustrate this is the rather embarrassing tale of the young female executive who was sitting next to the company chairman at an important corporate dinner. She was so used to having dinner with her children that she automatically lent over to the chairman's plate and cut up all his food for him. This behaviour was perfectly appropriate for her role as a mum, but not for her role as a company employee.

More recently, the approach that different beliefs and actions are outworkings of different roles that we play was illustrated in the film *My Summer of Love*.[7] In this movie the main character Mona is torn between her brother Phil, a violent criminal who has become a Christian, and her new friend Tamsin, a rich private-school pupil who has adopted the thinking of the philosopher Nietzsche (who called himself the anti-Christ). While Phil prays for Mona, Tamsin leads her into a life of passionate experimentation and libertarianism. But in the climax of the film, Mona discovers that both Tamsin and Phil were only playing temporary roles for a short while: Phil gives up his faith and returns to his violent ways, whilst Tamsin goes back to school as a dutiful and submissive pupil.

Again one can trace the roots of this approach in the thinking of past philosophers and its shoots in today's world. This approach has roots in the work of Lev Vygotsky (1896–1934)[8] and is affected by the work of Michel Maffesoli. Vygotsky, a Soviet psychologist, argued that intellectual development is a function of human communities, rather than of individuals. Focusing particularly on the mental development of children, Vygotsky emphasized the importance of social interaction as a means of internalizing the shared knowledge of the culture. According to this social construct theory, our beliefs are constructed through our involvement in our culture.

But what happens if we don't actually live in one static culture, but in many, changing, subcultures? That is the question considered by the French sociologist Michel Maffesoli,[9] and developed by the British sociologist Zygmunt Bauman.[10] They argue that we live in a time of 'neo-tribes'. Whereas traditionally people may have lived in one static tribe, now we flit in and out of many groupings of people with whom we associate for a temporary, fragile period. Applying this to Vygotsky's idea means that, if our knowledge and understanding develop from our interaction with our cultural community, then in a culture of neo-tribes we will develop different beliefs at different times in our different sub-groupings.

So there we have two philosophical approaches, each rooted in academic thinking and each expressed in popular films. And both of them lead to the elevation of indiscriminate tolerance in our popular culture – which has an impact upon our conversations about the Christian gospel. Thus, when we talk about our faith in Christ, people will often reply, 'That's just your personal view,' or, 'That's just the phase you're going through.' Those who say, 'That's just your personal view,' appear to be demonstrating how much they have adopted the approach that our view of truth is just a personal perspective. They may not have heard of Hume or postmodern historical theory, and they may not have seen the film *Hero*, but they still seem to be influenced by their approach. Then, those who say, 'That's just the phase you're going through,' appear to be demonstrating how much they have adopted the approach that our view of truth is socially constructed and variable. They may not have heard of Vygotsky or Maffesoli, and they may not have seen the film *My Summer of Love*, but they still seem to be influenced by their approach.

So all Christians who want to help others to explore the Christian faith, whether we are talking from a pulpit or over the garden fence, will want to understand these approaches and know how to respond to them.

Responding Thoughtfully

There is no doubt that we all have different perceptions of reality. But that does not necessarily mean that there is no actual reality which exists independent of our perception. Indeed, even in the classic elephant story there was actually a real elephant that existed regardless of what any of the blind people thought. If they had not been blind then they would have been able to see it.[11] Perhaps we need to help people to consider whether it might be possible that there is a bigger picture out there that we can't see because we are 'spiritually blind'. Perhaps if we could have our eyes opened, then we would see a bigger reality. But that would only be possible if there was a God who could open our eyes and reveal his truth to us.

There is no doubt that we all play different roles in our lives. And most of us do go through different phases of belief. But that does not necessarily mean that there is no one truth that is true for all phases of our life. Perhaps, for example, there is a universal truth that all human beings are created for a love-relationship with God and with other people. Of course, that would only be possible if there were an all-loving God, and if that God provided some way to call us into a loving relationship with himself.

Taking these two together, then, it might be reasonable to consider whether there is a God who has revealed his truth and his love to us. If people will explore that question they will find that the answer is to be found in Jesus. However, they will also discover that this Jesus made absolute and exclusive truth claims. For example, when he gave us the good news that he came so that we might know God's truth and enter into his life, he added on the claim that he is the only way to know that truth and enter that life. This is recorded in John 14:6 where Jesus says, 'I am the way, the truth, and the life. No one can come to the Father except through me.' When I point people to those words, I am always careful to make it clear that this is not me making that exclusive claim; it is Jesus. I am simply reporting what he says and inviting them to consider it for themselves. I am not trying to force them to accept my belief. I am simply inviting them to look at the life and teaching of Jesus. If he is who he claims to be, God become human, then we must listen to what he says. Similarly, I am not trying to stop other people from expressing their opinion. It is good to listen to others, even those who state the opposite to Jesus. How else would we know whether or not to agree with them? Thus, I want to help people to listen to different views and to consider them – as long as they do the same with the life and teaching of Jesus.

That, it seems to me, is what true tolerance is. The Macmillan *Encyclopedia of Philosophy* (which takes up seven inches of many philosopher's bookshelves) defines toleration as 'the patient forbearance in the presence of something which is disliked or disapproved of.'[12] It is not accepting every view as equally true. Tolerance assumes disapproval – it cannot require us to approve of a view with which we disagree. But tolerance does mean that we recognize other people's right to hold different views – we even protect their right to express them. And, in that context, we have the right to encourage people to hear the message of Jesus who claims to bring true life – even though he carries with him the exclusive truth claim to be the only way to that life.

Notes

[1] Stephanie Holmes, 'Profile: Rocco Buttiglione', BBC News, 21 October 2004 – news.bbc.co.uk/2/hi/europe/3718210.stm
[2] Stephanie Holmes, 'Profile: Rocco Buttiglione'
[3] For a fuller outline of the plot see chapter 5 (p. 57), and for further discussion of the film's content see chapter 4 (p. 49).
[4] www.savedmovie.com
[5] National Secular Society press release: 'BBC Must stand firm against religious bullies', 6 January 2005 – www.secularism.org.uk/index.php?option=content&task=view&id=206&Itemid=31
[6] 'Jet Li Our Hero', *World Movie Magazine*, 23 September 2004 – www.worldmoviemag.com
[7] Written and directed by Pawel Pawlikowsky (BBC Films, 2004), based on the novel by Helen Cross (Bloomsbury, 2002). For a study guide on this film, go to www.damaris.org/content/content.php?type=1&id=257
[8] For more information on Lev Vygotsky, see www.wikipedia.org/wiki/Lev_Vygotsky
[9] See Michel Maffesoli, *The Time of Tribes: Decline of Individualism in Mass Society* (Sage Publications, 1995)
[10] For more information, see www.wikipedia.org/wiki/Zygmunt_Bauman
[11] In fact, this is really true of *Hero* too – the three versions of the story are not equally valid. The king tells his version

because he disbelieves Nameless, not because his story is equally valid. The third version, again told by Nameless, contradicts the king's at certain points because he is now, apparently, telling the true story.

[12] Maurice Cranston, 'Toleration' in *The Encyclopedia of Philosophy* (ed. Paul Edwards) (Macmillan, 1967), Vol. 8 p. 143

When issues of morality are very murky, if you don't have a strong definition of right and wrong, you can get lost.

Amanda Donahoe

2. All Inclusive – A Biblical Perspective on Tolerance

Tony Watkins

There was a time, not too long ago, when the vast majority of British people thought that Christianity occupied the moral high ground. But now Christians are viewed with contempt because we dare to insist on absolute truth and on absolute standards of right and wrong. The trouble is that historically orthodox Christians believe and, more to the point, *proclaim* that Jesus Christ is the only way by which people can come to know God. And Christians believe there are moral absolutes – especially in the area of sex and relationships. We are accused of being arrogant, bigoted and intolerant. And intolerance, in the eyes of our culture, is deeply immoral. It's religious fascism.

The preoccupation with rights in our culture leads to a concern that people should not be discriminated against on the basis of their ethnic background, gender, lifestyle or religion. And rightly so – discrimination is not acceptable. But many people see proclaiming the gospel as disparaging of other people and their faiths – it suggests that we think they are second class citizens, and so we are seen to discriminate. And making exclusive truth claims looks like cultural imperialism to some people. Obviously our diverse society must be able to function peacefully, regardless of the wide variety of religious views and lifestyles within it. But it is easy to move from being aware of that need for *fairness* to believing that all worldviews and all lifestyles are equally *valid*. As Lesslie Newbigin wrote:

> 'It has become commonplace to say that we live in a pluralist society – not merely a society which is in fact plural in the variety of cultures, religions and lifestyles which it embraces, but pluralist in the sense that this plurality is celebrated as a thing to be approved and cherished.'[1]

It is very uncomfortable to be accused of intolerance and arrogance, and we are often tempted to play down the uniqueness of Christ and to soft pedal on morality. Nearly thirty years ago, sociologist Peter Berger said that cultures have what he calls 'plausibility structures'[2] – deep rooted ways of thinking that make some ideas seem reasonable and others unthinkable. The current plausibility structures of our culture make the Christian belief in the uniqueness of Christ utterly inconceivable for most people. This is so strong within our society that it even becomes hard for Christians to keep the courage of their convictions. When we come to passages like the early chapters of Joshua describing the invasion of Canaan, we feel distinctly awkward, knowing how bad this looks to the people around us.[3]

But none of this is new. The context in which the apostle Paul did much of his evangelism was remarkably similar. The world of his day, under the influence of Greek and Roman cultures, was incredibly pluralist with the worship of many different gods competing in the marketplace. In Athens he was 'deeply troubled by all the idols he saw everywhere' (Acts 17:16). He found such a variety of objects of worship that there was even an altar to an unknown god (17:23). The pressure was on Christians to keep quiet about their faith, as in Ephesus (Acts 19:23f). Michael Green writes:

> '... the early Christians, making as they did ultimate claims for Jesus, met the problem of other faiths head-on from the very outset.... They did not denounce other faiths. They simply proclaimed Jesus with all the power and persuasiveness at their disposal.'[4]

If, like the early Christians, we are to remain true to our faith in a pluralist world, it is vital that we understand what the Bible says on these issues – especially the uniqueness of Christ – and that we have a proper understanding of tolerance.

Jesus uniquely reveals God to us

Pluralists are those who believe that all worldviews are valid, and that none of them should make exclusive claims. They claim that all religions – including Christianity – are nothing more than human understandings of Ultimate Reality. They assume that they can see what we can't – that all religious paths lead to the same goal, the same Ultimate Reality. Pluralists are quick to accuse Christians of arrogance, but *their* position is inherently arrogant – they make *themselves* the highest authority by which to judge everything else. The Christian understanding, by contrast, is that we cannot discover God by ourselves.[5] Since God is spirit, and therefore beyond what we can know through our physical senses, we cannot know him unless he reveals himself to us. Since God is infinite, we cannot possibly understand him except in so far as he discloses himself to us. That is what we believe is happening in Scripture and, supremely, in the person of Jesus Christ. Jesus is unique because he perfectly reveals God to us:

> 'I am the way, the truth, and the life. No one can come to the Father except through me.... Anyone who has seen me has seen the Father!' (John 14:6, 9)

Paul writes:

> 'Christ is the visible image of the invisible God.' (Colossians 1:15)

And in Hebrews we read:

> 'The Son reflects God's own glory, and everything about him represents God exactly.' (Hebrews 1:3)

Martin Luther wrote:

> 'God does not want to be known except through Christ, nor can he be known in any other way.... Christ alone is the means, the life, and the mirror through which we see God and know his will.'[6]

So our understanding of God is shaped not by what we want him to be like, but by how he has revealed himself to us. Whether or not that sits comfortably with our world, it's not within our power to do anything about it. We do not have the liberty to remake God into our image. We try, of course, because we're fallen human beings. But our task is to keep on submitting ourselves to what God has revealed of himself so that we gradually come to know him as he wishes to be known. The authority for Christian truth claims, then, does not lie with us and our human reason, but with what God has revealed.

The particular historical context of this revelation is a problem for some people, of course. How could God reveal himself through just one man or even one nation? What's so special about them anyway? Isn't the Bible (or Jesus) just one of many specific cultural expressions of the general human search for God?

The assumption behind this is that universal truths are more important than any truth which comes through particular historical events. The timeless propositions of Confucianism seem preferable to the nitty gritty, sometimes distasteful historical narratives of the Bible. But Vinoth Ramachandran points out that:

> '... the universal is always mediated through the particular, in the biblical scheme of things. This resonates with our experience of all artistic, literary and scientific achievement. It simply does not follow ... that just because all our thoughts, including our thoughts about God, are historically shaped, none of our thoughts can be true for all time and for all peoples. We can read *Hamlet* and recognize that Shakespeare is speaking to a human condition that is shared by people of all ages and cultures, while also freely acknowledging that it could never have been written in the way it was if Shakespeare had been living in 1950, or even in 1750. Similarly, the universal validity of Einstein's theories of Special and General Relativity is unquestioned in scientific circles; and the fact that he was a German Jew, or that his theories could never have emerged at an earlier time in the history of physics, do not impugn that universality.'[7]

The fact that Christ came to a specific time and place shows that God is prepared to accommodate himself to our limited minds in order to reveal himself. So now Jesus is the centre of our worship. Christians are people who have come into a relationship with God through Jesus Christ, and we worship Christ as God. It's not something which was dreamt up by the early church, but was the natural response of the first Christians to the risen Lord Jesus (Matthew 28:9, 17; John 20:28).

Jesus' Unique Moral Authority

Pluralists are often happy to see Jesus of Nazareth as a great example for us – but nothing more. In his life and death he was an example of love for others, forgiveness, reconciliation, the importance of having a strong sense of identity, integrity, and so on. Well yes, Jesus did exemplify such things, but he was much *more* than an example. Why did he need to die such a cruel death if he just wanted to be an example? Viewing Jesus in this way seriously diminishes him. Again, those who attack the Christian conviction in the uniqueness of Christ put their own reasoning as the highest authority. For them, Jesus has authority only in as far as he reflects the general view of what is right and wrong. But Jesus doesn't simply reflect moral values which we know about from elsewhere; he is radically different from other human beings in that he has inherent moral authority (e.g. Matthew 5:21–48). Jesus *is* our example, but he is not *just* an example. Once we become Christians, the process of becoming like Christ starts. It is something we work at, but more significantly it is something which *God* works at within us:

> 'For God is working in you, giving you the desire to obey him and the power to do what pleases him.' (Philippians 2:13)

Alister McGrath writes:

> 'When Paul urges his readers to be imitators of Christ, as he is (1 Corinthians 11:1), his words seem to suggest that being a Christian is to enter into so close and deep a relationship with Christ that believers in some way begin to imitate him in consequence of that relationship. Imitation is thus the fruit, not the precondition, of faith. To become a Christian is to begin the process, not so much of *conforming*, as of *being conformed*, to Christ. It is not so much we who are active, as God who is active, in this process.'[8]

Jesus' authority is not based on any human criteria. We don't claim that he speaks with authority because we can see the sense in what he says. Quite the reverse, in fact. We are so convinced of his innate authority that we assess *other* ideas on the basis of how well they fit with what *he* said. So, because evangelicals believe that Jesus has 'all authority' (Matthew 28:18), we believe that we must be faithful to what the New Testament says about him. The message is not our invention, which we are arrogantly imposing on people; it is a message from God to everyone about his extraordinary grace.

Jesus the Unique Saviour

Viewing Jesus as merely a good moral example and a good moral teacher doesn't only diminish Christ, it is also a badly flawed understanding of human nature. It ignores the real nature of the human predicament – that we have a fundamental bias towards putting ourselves at the centre of our worlds. We are incapable of following his example and making ourselves like him. This is grounded in the first three chapters of

Genesis, which are crucial for a genuinely Christian worldview.

God made human beings in his image (Genesis 1:26–28) – we are like him and were made for a relationship with him. Genesis 3 tells the tragic story of how everything changed. We still bear God's image, but our rebellion has twisted and corrupted it. So we live in a world of alienation – from God, each other, our environment and even ourselves. We live in a world of fear and shame and lies. And we are under God's judgement. Incredibly, God still cares for his image bearers, and we see the first sign of God's grace as he seeks out the newly fallen couple, calling, 'Where are you?' (Genesis 3:9). And we see the first hint that God will sort this mess out (Genesis 3:15). The rest of the Bible is the unfolding story of God's judgement *and* grace until, finally, we see a stunning picture of redeemed people back in relationship with God in the new heavens and new earth.

Because we were made for a relationship with God, there is something in us which longs for him. The writer of Ecclesiastes says that God 'has planted eternity in the human heart' (3:11). Paul says that God's creation of humanity, and his dealings with us, were with the express purpose of people seeking him, reaching out for him and finding him (Acts 17:27). It is a mark of God's grace that we do still feel that urge to know him. Perhaps the most fundamental human impulse we have is to worship. But if it cannot find its true expression – through a relationship with Jesus Christ – it creates substitutes (Romans 1:23). If we cannot worship God in spirit and truth (John 4:24) we will worship something else, whether it be idols, false ideas of God, ourselves or whatever. But because they are substitutes, we are left with a lingering feeling of emptiness and of longing.

All Inclusive – A Biblical Perspective on Tolerance

Why do we settle for substitutes? As well as the urge to know God, we are also rebels wanting to run away from him. It is easier to settle for partially fulfilling our desire to worship rather than face the full implications of encountering God himself. Besides which, we are blinded to 'the glorious light of the Good News' (2 Corinthians 4:4).

So we were created to know God, yet our sin makes it impossible. This brings us to the very heart of the Christian faith – and the most fundamental point of disagreement between Christianity and every other worldview. The religious impulse in human beings sets us on a quest to know God – a quest which has many different forms of expression but which nevertheless do all have a search for ultimate reality at their core. However, the Christian conviction is that the God of grace seeks for us. He makes all the running, revealing himself and repairing the broken relationship through the giving of the Son by the Father, and the self-giving of the Son in his crucifixion. There is no alternative (John 14:6).

Therefore, the New Testament insists that the task of the church and of individual Christians is to proclaim the good news of Jesus Christ. He is our message (Galatians 1:16) – his coming into our world, his death and his resurrection at a particular moment in history. But while the good news is very specific in its content (to the annoyance of pluralists), it is universal in its reach – an *exclusive* claim but an *inclusive* invitation. This is good news for everyone from every culture, every people group, every background, every circumstance.

To proclaim him, then, is not intolerance, but is a natural result of our conviction that the message is good news and is true for everyone – God is inviting people to know him, rather than settle for a substitute.

If Jesus is God's Son, then we have to speak up about him. If he is not, if he is just another guy – a good one, but in essence just the same as the rest of us – we have no message to proclaim. The authority for seeing him in these terms is not our own but that of the Bible – this is how Scripture sees him.[9] The New Testament is also clear that the message demands a response from people. The purpose of proclaiming God's great invitation is that people respond to it and are reconciled to him (2 Corinthians 5:18–20). So Paul, working in a very pluralist context, saw it as entirely appropriate to be *persuading* people (Acts 17:2–3, 17; 18:4). He refused to back down regardless of the insults or risks to his life (2 Corinthians 11:23–27). And he was adamantly unashamed about it:

> 'For I am not ashamed of this Good News about Christ. It is the power of God at work, saving everyone who believes – Jews first and also Gentiles.' (Romans 1:16)

Moral Absolutes

If God has created human beings to live in relationship with him, and if Scripture is God's revelation of himself, then it follows that we must take the moral and ethical frameworks of the Bible very seriously. The Bible is unequivocal that there are moral standards which do apply to all humanity, whether or not people choose to accept them (see Romans 2:6–16, for example).

But it is not just clear moral commands that we must think about. We also need to take seriously the moral structure of the world God has created, in particular (in this context) the structure of marriage. The traditional

Christian opposition to homosexual activity is not primarily because of biblical texts which prohibit it – there are not that many passages which mention it explicitly, and some of them do have significant difficulties in interpretation. The orthodox Christian view has a much more fundamental basis: it is that in the Bible there is a clear pattern for sexual relationships – one man and one woman together for life in an unbreakable, covenantal relationship (Genesis 2:24). *Any* sexual relationship outside of this pattern, whether homosexual or heterosexual, is a departure from the moral structure of the world as God has made it. We may or may not like it, but if God has made it that way, we are not in fact in a position to argue.

The particular pattern of marriage is also profoundly significant because it is meant to be a lived metaphor for the relationship between God and his people (Ephesians 5:31–32). It is a relationship grounded in both similarity and difference, and which is characterised by extraordinary intimacy and exclusive commitment. If we allow our sexual relationships to divert from the pattern, instead of modelling this relationship, we will be modelling the spiritual unfaithfulness and waywardness of human beings, as the prophets stress so forcefully (see, for example, Jeremiah 2:20–25; 3:1–5; Hosea 1–3).

Christians believe that, because God has created us in his image, it is best for us to live according to his pattern – that is, living in a way which is consistent with his character as he has revealed himself. Not only is it best for us to live this way, but we also have a moral obligation to obey our creator (e.g. Exodus 20). And more than that, knowing that we are the bride of Christ, bought by his death on the cross, we long to be ready for him (Revelation 21:2); we long to be conformed to his likeness. So we will not back down on moral issues.

But it is one thing for Christian believers to be convinced of these things, it is another thing entirely to force these perspectives on unbelievers around us. If they do not acknowledge God as Lord of all, how can we expect them to live in obedience to him? Could we live in obedience to him before we became Christians? We need to recognise that without the Holy Spirit at work in someone's life, genuinely godly living is impossible. So we should not pressurise non-Christians into conforming – it can cause an unwanted backlash which leads to the Gospel itself being rejected.

However, we can argue that the morality set out in the Bible *makes sense*. We can point to practical advantages of living this way, and the negative effects of living in other ways. In the context of sexual relationships, the advantages of marriage are fantastic – security, trust, openness, stability for children, etc.[10] And the negative effects of living outside the pattern are enormous: the emotional trauma of relationship breakdown (far more likely when there isn't the same level of commitment), the risk of sexually transmitted infections, unwanted pregnancies, etc.

It is also legitimate for us to point out that we believe this is the best way for human beings to live, because we believe that this is how God created us. But the plausibility structures of our society are such that few people will pay much attention – unless they can see real benefits in our lives that result from us sticking with God's pattern. So it is crucial for Christians to be living lives of the highest moral standards – and helping each other to do so – but we must act towards others with grace, not judgementalism (1 Corinthians 5:9–13). A combination of godly living (Titus 2:11–13) and grace in our conversations with people (Colossians 4:6) can be very powerful, and it doesn't come across as intolerance.

True Tolerance

As Nick Pollard points out in the previous chapter, tolerance is not – as most people seem to think – a willing acceptance or a celebration of every perspective. On the contrary, the concept of tolerance *only* makes any sense if there is disapproval. We may disagree profoundly with someone else's beliefs or lifestyle, but we respect their right to choose for themselves. We may urge them to reconsider, we may even point out that they are accountable to God, but we should neither coerce nor pressurise people into changing.

In contrast to the prevailing view, tolerance is, in fact, a Christian virtue. It is grounded in our beliefs about the nature of human beings – created in God's image yet rebels against him. Since everyone is created by God, each of us is given the freedom to choose to obey God or to rebel against him (Joshua 24:15). Each of us is personally accountable before God for the choices we make. That means we must respect the choices people make. If God gives us the individual responsibility of choosing our path through life, we must respect someone's choices even when we don't like them.

The Christian view of human beings also drives us to be inclusive and accepting in our dealings with people – an attitude that is far from intolerance. God who is concerned for the outcasts expects us to be the same. In the Old Testament, Israel was commanded to be welcoming and generous to foreigners, the poor, widows and others on the fringes of society (Leviticus 19:10,

33, 34; Deuteronomy 14:28–30). In the New Testament, Jesus was also concerned for the marginalised (e.g. Luke 5:12–13; 7:11–15, 36–50; 8:43–48) and for people beyond the boundaries of Israel (John 10:16). Christians should have the same attitude: being inclusive, not showing favouritism (Leviticus 19:15; James 2:1–4) because everyone we encounter bears the image of God and is loved by him. It should be Christians who are leading the way in social inclusion – it would help to undermine the view of the church as exclusivist.

The fact that people are created by God also means we take seriously their quest to discover him. And the fact that they are rebels means their search is taking them in a wrong direction. We must empathise with the dead ends down which their search has taken them, because we, too, are rebels and have been down dead ends. It means we respect their rationality, which is a gift of God and which enables them to discover things that are right and true. Fallen they may be, but that doesn't mean that they can't find some truth. In fact, they may well discover things that are right and true which we may have missed. We may base our Christian worldview on God's authoritative word, but our understanding of it is far from perfect, and we still struggle with the ongoing reality of a fallen nature which twists some truth to our own purposes, and blinds us to other truths. So we should have a genuine humility in all our dealings with others, open to what we can learn from them as well as eager to share our knowledge of God with them.

As Christians, we must be crystal clear that Jesus is not simply *our* Lord, but *the* Lord, and that the most crucial question to ask is, 'Who do you say Jesus is?' We must be clear that we have the standards we do because that is how God has revealed himself. And we must be respectful of those who bear God's image, whatever they believe or do. We must be patient about the fruitless running after things that will not ultimately satisfy – that same longing may open them up to God's grace. Like Jesus, we need to be people who are characterised by grace and truth (John 1:14, 17) – committed to truth, acting in grace however people respond to us.

Notes

[1] Lesslie Newbigin, *The Gospel in a Pluralist Society* (SPCK, 1989), p. 1
[2] See for example, *The Heretical Imperative* (Doubleday, 1980)
[3] See David Couchman, 'God and the Canaanites' (www.bibletoday.co.uk/joshua6.htm) for some helpful material on this issue.
[4] Michael Green, *Acts for Today* (Hodder & Stoughton, 1993), p. 38
[5] Paul tells us that we can know something *about* him from the creation (Romans 1:20), but we cannot come to *know* God this way.
[6] Quoted in Alister McGrath, *A Passion for Truth* (Apollos, 1996), p. 37
[7] Vinoth Ramachandra, *Faiths in Conflict?* (IVP, 1999), p. 129
[8] Alister McGrath, *A Passion for Truth*, (Apollos, 1996) p. 44
[9] There are good reasons for believing the Bible, but this book isn't the place to go into them. A good starting point is Paul Barnett's *Is the New Testament Reliable?* (IVP, 2005).
[10] Of course, we live in a fallen, broken world and these aspects can at times be hard to find in a marriage – even a faithful one between Christians. But the difficulties and struggles are a reflection of our fallenness, not of the wisdom or otherwise of marriage itself. While it takes

genuine commitment and seriously hard work to make a marriage work, it is far more difficult to find these benefits in other sexual relationships.

This is England. You can do whatever you like.

Monica Ali, *Brick Lane*

3. Testing Tolerance

Tony Watkins

Everybody assumes that society is becoming increasingly tolerant – but is it? What kind of tolerance is it anyway? The latter part of 2004, and the early part of 2005 were interesting times in the ongoing debates about tolerance in the UK with controversies about television programmes and stage shows.

Protests Pay Off

In September 2004, the BBC cancelled a cartoon series called *Popetown* just before it was due to be shown on the digital channel BBC Three. The 2.4 million pound, ten part series was centred around an infantile pope (voiced by Ruby Wax) who bounces around the Vatican on a pogo stick, and morally dubious, scheming cardinals. Predictably it generated a considerable amount of opposition from Roman Catholics who were concerned that it would cause offence by its ridiculing of Catholicism. BBC Three controller Stuart Murphy pulled the plug on the basis that the risk of offence was very real and outweighed the artistic merits of the programme. In the words of the BBC Director-General Mark Thompson, 'the decision provoked an immediate outcry from some prominent secularists.'[1] He says they perceived a trend towards vocal religious groups pressurising the BBC and other bodies to back down over religious issues. Thompson referred to an article by David Aaronovitch in which he issued a rallying cry:

> 'It is time, as religion begins its comeback, for secularists to fight back. Not with bans . . . but with strong arguments and stronger alternatives.'[2]

Not long afterwards, the events of December 2004 confirmed the secularists' fears when Sikh protestors succeeded in getting the Birmingham Repertory Theatre to axe a play which they found offensive. *Behzti* (Dishonour), by Gurpreet Kaur Bhatti, was infuriating the Sikh community leaders because it included scenes of sexual abuse and rape inside a gurdwara (Sikh temple). It was this setting that caused the problems. Inderjit Singh wrote in the *Sikh Messenger* that 'it took all the nasty aspects of life, and put them in the holiest place, a temple, and that is grossly insulting.'[3] Sikh leaders pleaded for a rewrite so that the action took place in a community centre instead, but their requests were refused. Bhatti says:

> 'For a story to be truly universal, I think it is important to start with what is specific. Though the play is set in a gurdwara, its themes are not just about Sikhism, and I hope that a person of any faith, or indeed of no faith, could relate to its subject matter. I feel that the choice of setting was crucial and valid for the story I wanted to tell and, in my view, the production was respectful to Sikhism. It is only a shame that others have not had the chance to see it and judge for themselves.'[4]

The protests escalated into violence and the theatre stopped the run, claiming that it could no longer guarantee the safety of people coming to watch the play. Bhatti was forced into hiding after death threats were made against her and her family.

To those people with an agenda of moving Britain towards becoming increasingly secular, these two incidents were clear signs of the power of religious lobbies. They saw them as yet more evidence of the rise of various strains of fundamentalism – perhaps all the more so in the light of the influence wielded by the Christian Right in the recent American Presidential elections. According to the BBC's Director of Television Jana Bennett:

> 'A passionate debate challenging freedom of expression is under way on both sides of the Atlantic. Greater pressure is being placed on broadcasters and arts organisations than at any time I can recall in my media career. The debate in some cases has even been characterised by an undercurrent of intimidation and violence. We're in an age where multiculturalism, diversity and tolerance rub shoulders sometimes uneasily with freedom of expression.'[5]

Protest Ignored

More was to follow the following month with the BBC's planned broadcast of *Jerry Springer – The Opera*. A staggering 55,000[6] objections were sent to the BBC before transmission. The protest was intensified by emails and Christian websites urging people to make their feelings known. One group, Christian Voice,[7] went further and published the home addresses and telephone numbers of BBC executives, stating: 'We make no apologies for giving [these details] ... We know normal protests are channelled in such a way as to be ignored.'[8] The BBC took legal action to have the details removed, but claimed that staff and their families received 'a large number of abusive and unpleasant calls.'[9] Christian Voice director Stephen Green distanced himself from the abuse saying, 'We totally abhor stuff like that, it does no credit to the cause of Christ. But I was a bit naive in thinking perhaps our website would only be visited by Christians.'[10] Arguably he's also naive for thinking that no Christians would stoop to such indefensible behaviour. Terry Sanderson, vice president of the National Secular Society, accused Christians of being 'religious bullies' saying: 'This organised attack is the latest of a series of attempts by religious interests to control what we can see or say in this country.'[11] However, the Iona Community spoke for many uncomfortable Christians when it distanced itself from Christian Voice, calling it 'shrill and unrepresentative', and referring to its actions as 'attention-seeking and temper tantrums'.[12]

But, despite the storm of criticism, the BBC pressed ahead with the broadcast. It was delighted at the viewing figures of 1.7 million – significantly higher than the average of 1 million for regular opera productions. But there were thousands more complaints. The report of the BBC Governors' Programme Complaints Committee states that:

> 'Overall the night was the subject of over 65,000 communications with the BBC. Around 96% were complaints ... Over 84% preceded transmission and the purpose of those was, in general, to persuade the BBC not to transmit the programme.'[13]

In other words, around 10,000 people complained to the BBC after the broadcast. Never before had the BBC received this number of objections. But the complaints committee still concluded, by a majority of four to one, that the Corporation had been right to broadcast *Jerry Springer – The Opera*, and that the artistic merits of the show outweighed the offence it caused.

The secularists saw this as a victory – the tide of intolerance was being turned. Evangelical Christians viewed it somewhat differently. To them it felt like one more example of historically orthodox Christian faith being pushed to the margins of society and denied a voice. It seemed to some that, while there was no way a theatre dare stand against a vocal ethnic minority, the BBC felt safe to ignore protests from mainstream Christians. Given the responsibilities of the BBC,[14] the nature of the concerns, and the sheer number of complaints, the attitude of the BBC did strike many people as rather arrogant. It seemingly ignored the views of church leaders it had invited to discussions two days before the broadcast,[15] as well as those of large numbers of individual people. It also appeared that the BBC was breaching its commitments on offence, decency and taste as expressed in its formal agreement with the Government and in its Producers Guidelines. At the time of writing, the Christian Institute is awaiting the outcome of a judicial review into whether or not the BBC flouted these regulations.[16]

An Unlevel Playing Field?

An interesting question is whether or not the BBC would have acted in such an apparently high-handed way if another religion had been the focus of the ridicule. Respect towards religious and ethnic minorities is, rightly, a sensitive issue, but it often feels that Christianity is exempt. Instead it seems to be fair game for misrepresenting, parodying or ridiculing. On the *Culture Show* a few days after the broadcast, BBC Two Controller Roly Keating stepped around the question of whether the BBC would have shown *Jerry Springer – The Opera* if the character of Jesus in the show had instead been Muhammad, saying, 'Every work of art is different so you can never answer a question about a hypothetical and invented piece of art.'[17] He did go on to confirm, though, that he does believe it would be possible to 'combine extremely challenging satire, very extreme comic imagery, with other religions.' Tom Norris, associate director of the National Theatre, said:

> 'I don't think anyone should be stopped from doing satire on Islam, but I think that the creative community generally doesn't think that's the number one target. There's too much injustice and misunderstanding about that community already. I think the case of Christianity is different. I think we are essentially a Christian culture. Certainly the writers of *Jerry Springer – The Opera* have a lot of Christianity in their blood and heritage, and feel, therefore, that it's OK to explore that area bravely.'[18]

In other words, attacking core elements of Christian faith is fine because Britain has a Christian heritage. Political commentator Timothy Garton Ash argues that it is important to be even-handed in the treatment of all groups:

> '... because Britain is increasingly multicultural, all variations of religion, all "cultures" ... should get used to living with a higher degree of public offence. Either

you try to protect everyone from offence, or you allow offence equally for all. I'm emphatically of the offence-to-all persuasion.'[19]

Blasphemy

The central issue for Christians was the blasphemy. Although few protestors had seen the show, the content had been summarised in reviews of the stage production. Co-writer Stewart Lee, however, says:

> 'I'm not religious, but I wouldn't want people offended by this opera. There actually isn't a hint of blasphemy.'[20]

Mark Thompson – a practising Catholic – agreed, saying he 'believed there was nothing blasphemous in the production'.[21] Others tried to justify the broadcast on the grounds that blasphemy doesn't matter. The day before the show, Will Wyatt, former Managing Director of the BBC, discussed the show with the Evangelical Alliance's theological advisor David Hilborn on BBC1's *Breakfast*. He said: 'Times move on; the majority of the people in this country don't believe in God any more. The notion of blasphemy, I think, is rather an odd one to have in this day and age.'[22]

But after the broadcast, the spokesperson for the Church of England, Bishop of Manchester Nigel McCulloch, released a statement saying:

> 'My previously expressed concerns about some of its content being shown uncut on television (rather than in the theatre), especially by a public service broadcaster, are if anything, stronger. In particular, the brief scene in which Eve clearly attempts to masturbate Jesus (shown more closely by the television camera than would be the

case for the theatre audience) was gratuitously offensive and went beyond the boundary of taste and decency. Other words, especially those spoken to Jesus, together with audience reaction, crossed for me, as a television viewer, the boundary between satire and ridicule.'[23]

Christian Voice announced its intention to privately prosecute 'all responsible, from the Chairman of [BBC] Governors down to the stagehand at the Cambridge Theatre where it was recorded.'[24] Stephen Green says, 'Having seen the thing, if this is not blasphemy, nothing is. There will be nothing sacred if we cannot successfully prosecute the BBC.'[25] Antony Pitts, a senior BBC Radio Three producer agreed with Green and McCullough and resigned on 12 January after watching the programme (urged by Mark Thompson to do so before taking any action). He said:

'Having now watched the show in its entirety and the hour-long introductory broadcast, my conclusion was that the blasphemy was far, far worse than even the most detailed news reports had led me to believe. ... I feel a corporate responsibility for what has happened – aggravated by the fact that we the BBC did not give sufficient attention to the overwhelming level of listener protest in advance.'[26]

However, the Governors' complaints committee concluded that:

'... there could be no doubt that these religious references were very extreme. As such, it was clear that these would cause offence and that that offence to some viewers would be genuine. The Television Compliance Form shows that the BBC fully realised this. The issue was whether these elements (and hence subsequent offence) could be justified on grounds of exceptional or outstanding quality or relevance . . .

'The BBC is committed to freedom of expression, and has a duty to innovate, to reflect new and challenging ideas, and to make available to its audiences work of outstanding artistic significance. In all the circumstances, the outstanding artistic significance of the programme outweighed the offence which it caused to some viewers and so the broadcasting of the programme was justified.'[27]

Freedom of Speech

Mark Thompson quotes a section of the BBC Producers' Guidelines which states that:

> 'the right to challenge audience expectations in surprising and innovative ways, when circumstances justify, must also be safeguarded.'[28]

David Hilborn produced a critique of *Jerry Springer – The Opera* for the Evangelical Alliance before the broadcast. Towards the end he makes the telling point that:

> 'Even if *Jerry Springer – The Opera* is meant as an attack on reality TV, celebrity culture and the rest, it offers nothing more positive in place of what it condemns. It uses biblical motifs for convenience, but mocks the redemption to which they point. Superficially, it is sardonic and witty. At heart, though, it is vacuous, gross and as cynical as its eponymous anti-hero. Make no mistake: its language, sexual content and blasphemy are all nauseating. But it is this vast moral emptiness which Christians should find most offensive of all.'[29]

And there, at the heart of all this, lies a paradox. The 'vast moral emptiness' of which Hilborn speaks gives rise to the offensive content – it follows easily when there are no checks or boundaries. Arguably, moral emptiness is a significant element of our culture today. Yet Christians are not constantly protesting against it. In fact, the Christian conviction that free speech and genuine tolerance are important would make us uphold the right of people to embrace moral emptiness even while profoundly disagreeing with their position (this is what tolerance really means, after all). On the other hand, we do believe that society works best if it has a solid moral core, and that decency and respect for others' views are good for us all. I believe in freedom of expression, and I believe in tolerance of people who say things I profoundly disagree with, or who attack my beliefs. I have no problem with the right of people to advocate atheism or other worldviews on the BBC – ultimately the truth can stand for itself. But when the very centre of our faith is so offensively ridiculed in such an extreme way, it seems to me that those who are claiming the right to freedom of expression are neglecting the responsibilities which go with it.

In a statement about the *Behzti* affair, Don Horrocks, Head of Public Affairs with the Evangelical Alliance, said:

> 'There is no doubt that with artistic freedom there should come responsibility. It is not acceptable to cloak religious provocation and insult under the guise of artistic license – that would amount to a form of "religious fundamentalism" in itself. On the other hand, the correct response to provocation should not be coercive censorship. In this country we have the freedom to express ideas, many of them controversial, which is a precious liberty that should be preserved. Peaceful protest and challenge,

combined with boycotting and critique is the most acceptable way to express opposition.'[30]

If we believe that truth can stand for itself we have no reason to adopt a defensive stance in order to protect ourselves. That will mean we are offended at times, and we ought to be able to live with that. But there are degrees of offence, and sometimes we can legitimately feel that things have gone too far. Where that line is will be different for different people – some people are less easily offended than others. The law as it stands is clear about the need for 'decent and temperate language'[31] and it is entirely reasonable to protest when we believe that something has gone too far, or the language used is not decent or temperate – providing that our protesting does not itself go too far. We, too, need to be decent and temperate and not bring the gospel into disrepute by our actions and words.

Notes

[1] Mark Thompson, 'Stationers' Livery Lecture given in London – Angels and Emails', 7 March 2005 – www.bbc.co.uk/pressoffice/speeches/stories/thompson_livery.shtml

[2] David Aaronovitch, 'Flaws of Faith', *The Observer*, 26 September 2004 – observer.guardian.co.uk/comment/story/0,,1312826,00.html

[3] Quoted in Alex Sierz, 'Dispatches: Holy Offensive', *Believe it or not* – www.channel4.com/culture/microsites/B/believeitornot/debates/holyoffensive.html

[4] Gurpreet Kaur Bhatti, 'This warrior is fighting on', *The Guardian*, 13 January 2005 – www.guardian.co.uk/comment/story/0,,1389198,00.html

[5] Jana Bennett, 'We cannot be ruled by Pop Idol protests', *The Guardian*, 28 February 2005 – www.guardian.co.uk/comment/story/0,,1426744,00.html

6. 'BBC rejects Springer complaints', BBC News, 30 March 2005 – news.bbc.co.uk/1/hi/entertainment/tv_and_radio/4393533.stm
7. www.christianvoice.org.uk
8. *Independent on Sunday*, 9 January 2005
9. 'Group to act over Springer opera', BBC News, 10 January 2005 – news.bbc.co.uk/1/hi/entertainment/tv_and_radio/4161109.stm
10. 'Group to act over Springer opera', BBC News
11. 'BBC must stand firm against religious bullies', 6 January 2005 – www.secularism.org.uk/index.php?option=content& task=view&id=206&Itemid=31
12. Kathy Galloway, 'Not a very Christian voice', *The Guardian*, 9 March 2005 – www.guardian.co.uk/letters/story/0,3604,1433393,00.html
13. 'Finding by the Governors' Programme Complaints Committee, *Jerry Springer – The Opera*, BBC Two, Saturday 8 January 2005' – news.bbc.co.uk/1/shared/bsp/hi/pdfs/30_03_05_jerryspringer.pdf
14. See Tony Watkins, 'Jerry Springer – The Opera' – www.damaris.org/content/content.php?type=5&id=396
15. You can read the statement issued after the meeting by the Churches Media Council (7 January 2005) at www.churchesmediacouncil.org.uk/docs/press/2005/general/20050107%20Springer%20statement.pdf
16. 'BBC to face the High Court following Jerry Springer opera', 19 January 2005 – www.christian.org.uk/pressreleases/2005/january_19_2005.htm
17. *The Culture Show*, BBC Two, 13 January 2005
18. *The Culture Show*
19. Timothy Garton Ash, 'In praise of blasphemy', *The Guardian*, 13 January 2005 – www.guardian.co.uk/print/0,3858,5102165-103677,00.html
20. www.stewartlee.co.uk
21. 'Protests as BBC screens Springer', BBC News, 10 January 2005 – news.bbc.co.uk/1/hi/entertainment/tv_and_radio/4154071.stm

[22] You can watch the video of the discussion at news.bbc.co.uk/media/video/40698000/rm/_40698149_jerry_disco_vi.ram

[23] www.manchesteronline.co.uk/news/s/142/142249_bishop_joins_protest_over_springer_opera.html

[24] www.christianvoice.org.uk/Springer1.html

[25] 'Springer opera draws 1.7m viewers', BBC News, 9 January 2005 – news.bbc.co.uk/1/hi/entertainment/tv_and_radio/4159217.stm

[26] 'Antony Pitts' resignation letter', *The Guardian*, 12 January 2005 – media.guardian.co.uk/broadcast/story/0,7493,1388451,00.html

[27] 'Finding by the Governors' Programme Complaints Committee, *Jerry Springer – The Opera*, BBC Two, Saturday 8 January 2005' – news.bbc.co.uk/1/shared/bsp/hi/pdfs/30_03_05_jerryspringer.pdf

[28] Mark Thompson, 'Stationers' Livery Lecture given in London – Angels and Emails'

[29] David Hilborn, 'Jerry Springer, The Opera', 5 January 2005 – www.eauk.org/contentmanager/Content/press/statements/jerryspringer.cfm

[30] Don Horrocks, 'Evangelical Alliance rejects violent censorship', 23 December 2004 – www.eauk.org/contentmanager/Content/press/2004/12/23.cfm

[31] The proposed law against 'Incitement to Religious Hatred' has worried Christians and atheists alike on the basis that it might take away their freedom to criticise any religious belief or practice. However, a written statement from the Home Secretary David Blunkett states: 'The Government is committed to the preservation of the right to legitimate freedom of speech and freedom of religion. This includes the right to engage in free and vigorous debate about religion, including the right to criticise religious beliefs and practices. The Government also recognises that proselytism is an integral activity for many faith communities. Such debate, criticism and proselytism can be undertaken without using threatening, abusive or insulting behaviour

that is intended or likely to stir up hatred. Expressions of antipathy or dislike of particular religions or their adherents can also be made without crossing the thresholds of the offence. This provision will not restrict but protect people's legitimate freedom to practice their religion without fear.' (Home Office, 'Incitement to religious hatred' 7 December 2004 – www.homeoffice.gov.uk/docs4/incitement_wms7december.pdf)

I'm not a practising Catholic or I wouldn't be living unwed with a woman, and I don't think all poofs are going to hell, and I don't think everyone who's had an abortion is damned. Most of my friends are atheists and I understand atheism, I get it, but I happen to be a theist. I believe in our answerableness to something else.

Martin Freeman

4. Lip Service

Louise Crook

Saved![1] is a story of teenage angst and insecurity, of friendship and prejudice set in a Christian high school in America. It centres around a teenage girl, Mary (Jena Malone), who becomes confused about her faith after attempting to save her gay boyfriend (Chad Faust) by sleeping with him and becoming pregnant. What adds to her confusion is her treatment at the hands of Christians she had looked up to.[2]

Co-writers Brian Dannelly (who also directed) and Michael Urban both have experience of Christian fundamentalism. At Dannelly's Baptist high school, the rules were strict:

> 'In my high school, we weren't allowed to dance. Everybody had to be at least six inches away from the opposite sex at all times. We had record burnings, and the entertainment at my senior prom was a puppet show – it wasn't very exciting.'[3]

Urban, who grew up in a 'traditional Baptist home' in the southern USA, says:

'Where I went to college in Tallahassee, Florida, I regularly saw people who lived in this metaphysical world with punishments and demons and things I had a hard time understanding. Sometimes things are twisted and exploited in the name of religion or God. I wanted to explore that.'[4]

This aim does seem a worthy one – after all, hypocrisy is never a good thing and Christians must stand against it as much as anyone. However, the film does not stop at satirising hypocritical Christians, but seems to go much further and parodies all that evangelical Christians stand for. The Christians in *Saved!* make life difficult for everyone. Hilary Faye (Mandy Moore) is a good example of this. She loves to talk about Jesus and his saving power, and declares that 'I am filled with Christ's love.' Yet she treats her disabled brother Roland (Macaulay Culkin) with contempt, and instigates a hate campaign against her friend Mary to get her thrown out from school. She is full of bitterness rather than love, and seems inherently cruel. The adult Christians are no better. Pastor Skip (Martin Donovan) tries to present Jesus in an appealing way to his pupils, telling them to 'kick-it Jesus style' and seeks to give them moral guidance. However, he has given up on his marriage and embarks on an affair with Mary's mother Lillian (Mary-Louise Parker). The affair distracts him from serving his pupils effectively, and absorbs Lillian so much that she fails to notice her daughter is pregnant.

On the other hand, the non-Christian pupils at the school are presented in a far more positive light. Cassandra's rebellion against the school authorities and Christian ideals means she is portrayed as a breath of fresh air in an oppressive environment. Her love for Roland is in clear contrast to Hilary Faye who can't see beyond her brother's disability. It is Roland and Cassandra who support Mary in her time of need, while the Christians judge her and reject her outright. Mary is portrayed increasingly sympathetically as she moves away from her Christian roots and becomes more rebellious.

Saved! suggests that Hilary Faye and her cronies need to be saved from religion and the Christian establishment. It seems the filmmakers have set out to expose the faults of legalistic Christians who are steeped in hypocrisy, and are intolerant of those who do not live up to their moral standards. However, it would be unfair to accuse the film of rejecting Christian faith altogether. Indeed, the producers of the film have said that, 'the film does not criticize Christians, religion, or faith. The film speaks out against those who are intolerant and their inability to open their hearts and minds to others' way of thinking.'[5] At the end of the film, Mary has not lost her faith altogether. After the birth of her baby she says:

> 'Life is too amazing to be meaningless – there has to be God, something out there – you just have to feel it.'

What she does reject is the way of thinking that she has been taught by her Christian community. This film is very much a product of our postmodern age, suggesting that no one has a right to impose their views on others, and that everyone has to make their own truth.

Albeit unwittingly, *Saved!* is an exploration of human sin. Co-writer Michael Urban has obviously been much affected by how he saw Christians behaving as he was growing up. And the film is correct – Christians cannot live up to the standards that God has set for us. No human being can live up to God's perfect standards because we all reject him as the rightful ruler of our lives. Christians are often viewed as hypocrites because they set themselves and others high biblical moral standards that they just can't live up to. But how many people can even live up to their own standards? We fail to be the people we think we should be, and we seem to be incapable of bringing about much in the way of transformation on our own. However, the essence of the Christian message is not about living up to a set of moral standards; it is that we all need forgiveness for our rejection of God – we need Jesus. Only by accepting Jesus Christ into our lives can we have forgiveness and, therefore, a personal relationship with God. It is true that Christians do not live up to their calling to be perfect. However, this does not mean that what God has done for us through Jesus Christ should be mocked. God has revealed his awesome love for us by letting his Son die on our behalf, and this is something that demands a personal response from each one of us.

Saved! is a revealing insight into the secular opinion of American evangelicals. Christians need to wake up to society's perception of them as hypocritical and judgemental, a view which has, it seems, ultimately led the makers of this film to reject Christianity. This portrayal of Bible-believing Christians is in stark contrast to the great love that Jesus had for all the people he met. Jesus firmly rejected sin, but did not turn away from the sinner. My hope is that people who watch this film won't reject Christianity outright because of its portrayal of Christians, but instead will judge the Christian faith by looking at the incredible account of God and his love for humanity that can be found in the Bible.

However, *Saved!* also serves as a powerful reminder of the importance of integrity for Christians. Our inner reality must match up with our outward lives. The Pharisees of Jesus' time were thought to be shining examples of righteousness, but Jesus' assessment of them was that they were 'full of greed and wickedness' (Luke 11:39). His charges against them and against the experts in the Law were that they forgot the love of God and concern for others (Luke 11:42, 46), they were only concerned about outward show (Luke 11:43, 47) and they hindered others from coming into the kingdom (Luke 11:44, 52). Small wonder that Jesus warned his followers to, 'Beware of the yeast of the Pharisees – beware of their hypocrisy' (Luke 12:1). If we deal with the hypocrisy in our lives, we will be that much better at showing the grace of God through our lives.

Notes

[1] For background information on this film, see chapter 5 (p. 57)
[2] For a fuller plot summary, see chapter 5 (p. 57)
[3] www.savedmovie.com
[4] www.savedmovie.com
[5] www.savedmovie.com

I don't believe in organised religion, but I treat other people right and use the Ten Commandments ... well, I'm solid with eight or nine! That other people's wives thing just kills me!

Will Smith

5. *Saved!* – Study Guide

Louise Crook

Film Title: *Saved!*
Tagline: Heaven help us
Director: Brian Dannelly
Screenplay by: Brian Dannelly and Michael Urban
Starring: Jena Malone, Mandy Moore, Macaulay Culkin, Eva Amurri, Patrick Fugit, Mary-Louise Parker, Martin Donovan
Distributor: MGM
Theatrical Release Date: 29 October 2004
DVD Release Date: 28 February 2005
Certificate: 15

Keywords

Christianity, religion, hypocrisy, tolerance, acceptance

Summary

Mary Cummings (Jena Malone) introduces herself as a born-again Christian who has been following Jesus since the age of three. She lives with her mother (Mary-Louise Parker) and is just about to start her final year at American Eagle Christian High School, which is run by Pastor Skip (Martin Donovan). She is happy with her lot: she has Jesus at the centre of her life, is a member of a group of friends at school called the Christian Jewels, and has a perfect Christian boyfriend, Dean (Chad Faust). All seems to be going well for Mary.

That is, however, until she and Dean are in the swimming pool one day. They play a game which involves telling each other secrets while underwater. Dean tells Mary that he thinks he is gay. Shocked, Mary shoots up to the surface but hits her head on her ascent, and has what she believes is a vision of Jesus telling her to help Dean and cure him of his homosexual tendencies. After some deliberation, Mary decides that the best way to do this is to seduce him and so they sleep together. Soon afterwards, Dean's parents send him away to Mercy House to undergo a process of 'de-gayification'. Mary is very confused about her faith and what she has done – and becomes even more so when she discovers she is pregnant.

Mary keeps her pregnancy a secret; her best friend Hilary Faye (Mandy Moore) cannot understand Mary's change in behaviour. When the secret is discovered, Hilary Faye has little sympathy for her friend's plight. She seems more interested in attracting the attention of Pastor Skip's son Patrick (Patrick Fugit), recently returned from missionary work in South Africa and a world tour with the Christian Skateboarders Association.

So Mary turns elsewhere for friendship. Cassandra (Eva Amurri) is the school's only Jewish girl – she has been allowed into the school so that she can be saved. Cassandra guesses that Mary is pregnant and offers her a hand of friendship. Mary also strikes up a friendship with Roland (Macaulay Culkin), Hilary Faye's cynical, wheelchair-bound brother who has been shunned by his sister and others at the school because of his disability. Mary attracts the attention of Patrick who is prepared to accept her for who she is, and by the climax of the film on prom night, Mary feels more loved than she ever has before.

Background

Saved! has been steeped in controversy since its premier at the Sundance Film Festival in 2004. It is an all-American high school movie with the significant difference that it is set in a Christian high school and seems to parody such institutions. Co-writer Michael Urban was brought up in an evangelical Christian home and says he wanted to explore the way people distort things for the sake of their faith. *Saved!* achieved great success across the Atlantic, and did moderately well here in the UK. It managed to offend Christian and non-Christian critics alike, although some found its satire funny and accurate. Glenn Whipp wrote in the *Los Angeles Daily News:*

> 'The makers of *Saved!* want you to know that it's important to practice tolerance of others – unless, of course, those others are Christians. Then it's OK to mock, ridicule and reduce people to misshapen stereotypes because, well, they deserve it. The movie's hateful brand of reductive thinking will obviously be plenty offensive to believers. For others, *Saved!* will merely insult your intelligence in the usual depressing ways.'[1]

While in the *LA Weekly,* Ella Taylor wrote:

'Though *Saved!* is funny and irreverent, Dannelly isn't just taking potshots at fundamentalism. He creates a viable world, then riddles its surface piety with underground transgressions that call into question not Christian belief but slavish, intolerant religious practice.'[2]

Saved! is director and co-writer Brian Dannelly's first feature film. He was born in Germany, and moved to the US when he was eleven, attending a Catholic elementary school, a Jewish summer camp and a Baptist high school. He says:

'The biggest lesson I learned from my experience became a line in the script: "They can't all be wrong and they can't all be right."'[3]

He studied visual arts at university before becoming a directing fellow at the American Film Institute. The producer of the film is REM's singer/songwriter Michael Stipe who says:

'I thought it was one of the funnier and more absolutely audacious, subversive scripts I had seen in some time. I just fell in love with the characters and the story immediately.'[4]

Co-producer Sandy Stern insists that:

'the humour in the story is not meant to mock Christianity. We are not making fun of Christian people in this movie. Something is going on in the world right now that we haven't quite seen – Christianity has become a multi-billion dollar industry. ... With *Saved!* we're trying to show how teenagers are using religion as a way to cope in their day-to-day world.'[5]

Questions for Discussion

1. What did you think of the film? How did it make you feel?
2. With which character in *Saved!* do you most identify? Why?
3. Which characters does the film portray in a positive light? Which characters does it show up? Why have the film makers done this?
4. How would you describe the atmosphere at American Eagle Christian High School? Do you have any experience of this kind of atmosphere? How exaggerated would you say the portrayal of the school is?
5. 'In my high school, we weren't allowed to dance. Everybody had to be at least six inches from the opposite sex at all times. We had record burnings, and the entertainment at my senior prom was a puppet show – it wasn't very exciting.' (Brian Dannelly)

    'I regularly saw people who lived in this metaphysical world with punishments and demons and things I had a hard time understanding. Sometimes things are twisted and exploited in the name of religion or God. I wanted to explore that.' (Michael Urban)

    How do you think the childhood experiences of co-writers Michael Urban and Brian Dannelly have influenced the film? What impression does that give you of their childhoods?

6. What kind of person is Mary? What journey is she on during the film? What is it about her that attracts Patrick's attention?

7. What do you think Pastor Skip's relationship with Mary's mother Lillian adds to the story? Why do you think this subplot has been included?

8. How would you describe Hilary Faye as a character? How does she change as the film progresses? What do you think causes these changes? Is she a better person at the beginning or end of the film?

9. What do you think this film has to say about human nature? How does this fit with the biblical view of humanity (see Genesis 1:26–28; 3:1–20; Jeremiah 17:7–10)?

10. Why do the characters in the film treat each other so badly? Can you identify with this? What do you think the film is suggesting through the attitudes of the various characters towards each other? How does Galatians 5 relate to the situation?

11. Hilary Faye: 'Mary, turn away from Satan. Jesus, he loves you.'
    Mary: 'You don't know the first thing about love.'
    Hilary Faye [throwing a Bible at Mary]: 'I am FILLED with Christ's love! You are just jealous of my success in the Lord.'
    Mary [holding up the Bible]: 'This is not a weapon! You idiot.'

    How did this exchange make you feel? To what extent do you see similar attitudes reflected in your Christian community or in your own life? How are Hilary Faye's attitudes and actions measured by Isaiah 1:11–17 and Micah 6:7–8?

12. 'Belonging to [Christian groups] when they're teenagers can really motivate and unify today's young people. It brings such a sense of excitement and acceptance into their world and gives them a sense of community and security, which is very powerful. Our kids are growing up in a time of terrorism, AIDS, and classmates shooting up their schools. Teens are scared, and the Christian movement is something young people can be a part of and feel safe. It's a fantastic reflection of pop culture: everything cool in the secular world is mirrored in the Christian world. There's very little difference between the two now, and I think that's part of its appeal.' (Brian Dannelly)[6]

How does the film present Christianity? Do you think this presentation is fair? How do you respond to Dannelly's comments?

13. 'Life is too amazing to be a meaningless and random consequence of the Universe. There has to be a God, something out there – you just have to feel it.' (Mary)

'The film is absolutely pro-faith. It's about wanting to believe in something and the idea that belief and love can be in many different forms. It's not a matter of grouping into clean neat piles, but really understanding the chaos, understanding the debris on the side and knowing it's all part of the same thing.' (Jena Malone)[7]

Why does Mary come to this conclusion? To what extent do you agree with her comment? What kind of faith does Mary have at the end of the film? Do you feel that the film is opposed to Christian faith generally, or only to certain expressions of it? What else do you think Mary needs to understand, and what Bible passages would support it?

14. Pastor Skip: 'Patrick, this is not a grey area.'
    Patrick: 'Dad, it's all a grey area.'
    Pastor Skip: 'The Bible is black and white!'

    Do you agree with Pastor Skip? Why/why not? How does that kind of absolute certainty come across to the non-Christian world?

15. Cassandra: 'There's only one reason Christian girls come down to the Planned Parenthood [centre].'
    Roland: 'She's planting a pipe bomb?'
    Cassandra: 'Okay, two reasons.'

    What is *Saved!* suggesting about Christian intolerance? To what extent do you think it is fair? How should Christians respond to issues and people with whom we disagree (see 1 Corinthians 1:10–17; 5:9–13; 9:19–23; Ephesians 5:11–16)?

16. 'So everything that doesn't fit into some stupid idea of what you think God wants, you just try to hide or fix or get rid of? It's just all too much to live up to. No one fits in one hundred percent of the time. Not even you.' (Mary to Pastor Skip)

    How do you think your non-Christian friends feel about your attitudes to people who make a mess of their lives? How can we model God's grace in action in our dealings with other people (Mark 2:15–17; 2 Corinthians 6:3–13; Ephesians 2:1–10)?

17. When Mary is investigating different religions, she asks, 'Sure, they can't all be right, but surely they can't all be wrong?'

    Why do you think she says this? How would you respond to a friend who made this comment (see John 14:6–7; Acts 4:8–12)?

Notes

[1] Glenn Whipp, 'What would Jesus film? Nothing like this', *Los Angeles Daily News,* 26 May 2004 – u.dailynews.com/Stories/0,1413,211~24684~2173705,00.html
[2] Ella Taylor, 'Saved!', *LA Weekly* – www.laweekly.com/film/film_results.php?showid=2960
[3] www.savedmovie.com
[4] www.savedmovie.com
[5] www.savedmovie.com
[6] www.savedmovie.com
[7] www.savedmovie.com

Here's to the men who did what was considered wrong in order to do what they knew was right.

Ben Gates in the film *National Treasure*

6. *Hero* – Study Guide

Louise Griffiths

Film Title: *Hero* (Ying Xiong)
Tagline: This land doesn't know a real hero. Yet.
Director: Yimou Zhang
Screenplay by: Feng Li, Bin Wang and Yimou Zhang
Starring: Jet Li, Tony Leung Chiu Wai, Maggie Cheung, Ziyi Zhang, Daoming Chen, Donnie Yen
Distributor: Buena Vista
Theatrical Release Date: 24 September 2004
DVD Release Date: 21 February 2005
Certificate: 12

Key Words

Heroism, sacrifice, patriotism, truth, revenge

Summary

China in the third century BC is a divided land – a warring region of seven nations. However, one of the warring kings, Qin Shi Huangdi, (Daoming Chen) has great aspirations for a land of peace under one ruler – himself. He goes to war in order to bring peace and unity to the land, and the way to achieve the goal is by destroying any that fight against him. However, the king is a man who has no rest or tranquillity. His life has been in danger for years since he has gained many enemies during his crusades. He is guarded constantly by his highly trained and ruthless guards. No one can even get near him to attempt an assassination. Nevertheless, he still fears three deadly assassins in particular – Sky (Donnie Yen), Broken Sword (Tony Leung Chiu Wai) and his lover Flying Snow (Maggie Cheung) – who have been intent on killing him for many years. The king has lost many of his soldiers trying to track down and kill these three, but they are such skilled fighters that they seem to be invincible.

But now word reaches the king that one man has changed everything. He claims to have killed the three assassins. The king is surprised and suspicious, but he summons the man to his court to receive his rewards – vast amounts of gold and an audience alone with the king. The nameless warrior (Jet Li) is a local prefect – a very minor provincial official – in the land of Qin. He appears before the intrigued king with news of his part in the deaths of all three assassins. Nameless describes his first victory – the defeat of Sky, master of the spear – and then goes on to tell how he found the lovers Broken Sword and Flying Snow at a calligraphy school in the desert. By exploiting their jealousy towards one another, he divides them and kills them. As Nameless recounts each victory, he is allowed to come a little closer to the king who, it seems, is growing in his confidence in Nameless. But in fact, the king becomes deeply suspicious of this minor prefect succeeding where his own large forces had failed. He believes a different sequence of events must have occurred, and presents his version to Nameless. In response, Nameless gives a third account.

As the two men tell their different versions of the story, we see the events described through three series of distinctively coloured flashbacks – one predominant colour for each telling of the story: blue as we first see Nameless approach the King; red as he first tells his story; blue again as the king challenges Nameless' honesty; white when Nameless revises his account. Half-truths and truths become mixed and unclear; speculations and outright lies become combined. As the differing accounts are given, they begin to overwrite one another, and eventually the definitive truth is revealed.

Background

Director Yimou Zhang (*House of the Flying Daggers, The Road Home*) has raised the bar for Chinese Wushu films with *Hero*. The film was the most expensive Chinese film to be produced with the final cost at $30 million. It was essential to him to have a big star for the Chinese market, so Jet Li was cast as the nameless warrior. Li is a practising Buddhist and was excited about the project as he wanted to be involved in an action film with 'a positive message – that there are solutions other than violence.'

Yimou Zhang grew up with legends about attempts to assassinate the king who would become the first emperor of a united China. He says, 'We were told that there was an assassin from another district who pretended to the emperor that he wasn't an enemy anymore. He's in the emperor's court, holding a rolled-up map, and he wants to show the emperor where he comes from. But when he's unrolling the map, there's a knife inside. The emperor sees it, and has the assassin killed. I wanted to transform this story by giving it a different ending. We came up with two ways. One was that the assassin unrolls the map, but the knife isn't there.... Or we can work from the premise that the assassin decides not to kill the emperor. And that's how we decided to go.'[1]

Although *Ying Xiong* was released in China in 2002, the English version, *Hero,* was a hidden secret sitting on Miramax's shelf for two years before finally being released in America and Britain. Arguments between director Yimou Zhang and Miramax, along with concerns that it would not do well at the American box office, stalled the film's arrival in the west. Ironically, these delays had the effect of disproving those doubts: the film built up a significant following long before its American release, and it debuted at number one in the box office, taking $20 million in its opening weekend.

Zhang said: 'The modern concept of a hero is an everyday hero ... but in martial arts the hero is something unattainable – something that isn't humanly possible. It means someone who can run 10,000 miles without being seen, someone who can kill a man with every step he takes. That's the kind of thing that never happens in real life. So the martial arts hero is the opposite of the modern type: this kind of hero is just an impossible dream.'[2] The question that the film raises is: what makes a hero? *Hero* also addresses the topic of sacrifice within its exploration of heroism, as well as the interplay of different perspectives.

Questions for Discussion

1. What was your reaction to the film? What did you feel about the three different narratives and the ending? Why?

2. The different accounts of Nameless' encounters with the assassins are shot with different colours predominating. What is the significance of the different colours chosen for these different accounts? To what extent did the visual styling of the film affect you emotionally? To what extent did it affect you intellectually?

3. Within *Hero* a link is made between swordsmanship and both music and the art of calligraphy. What do you think this connection symbolises? What lessons can be learnt from this link? Why do you think this film has such an emphasis on beauty and grace?

4. The flashbacks within the film are all different perceptions on the same events. This is similar to the psychological position that we all see the same incident but from a different angle. Each of the flashbacks presented a different version of the 'truth'. How do you think this is reflected in society today? In *Hero* do you think any of the flashbacks is the real truth? What is the view of truth within the film? What relevance do Bible passages such as John 14:5–7 and John 18:33–38 have to this question?

5. What do you think motivates the assassins to want to kill the king? Do you think this is a good reason? Why/why not?

6. How is Broken Sword's relationship with Flying Snow portrayed in *Hero*? What do you think their relationship says about the nature of love?

7. The film is about one man becoming a hero. What do you think the film is saying about heroism? What do you think makes someone a hero? In what sense do the 'heroes of the faith' who are commended in Hebrews 11 deserve to be regarded as heroes?

8. How would you summarise the attitudes of Broken Sword, Flying Snow and Nameless towards the assassination of the King? Who do you most agree with? Why?

9. Nameless quotes Broken Sword, saying, 'One person's pain is nothing compared to the suffering of all.' What do you think Broken Sword meant by this statement? How would you compare this statement with Jesus' sacrifice to redeem the world (see John 10:11–18)?

10. In the Chinese version of the film, the closing credits say that the Chinese speak of their country as 'all under Heaven' (a poetic name for the nation, rather than the official name). But in the English version, it is instead translated as, 'Our Land'. In what ways does this alter the meaning? Which do you think is more powerful? Why? What do you think *Hero* is trying to say about patriotism?

11. 'Before China was one great country, it was divided into seven warring states. In the Kingdom of Qin was a ruthless ruler. He had a vision – to unite the land, to put an end, once and for all, to war. It was an idea soaked in the blood of his enemies.' (title cards)

'The people have suffered years of warfare. Only the King of Qin can stop the chaos by uniting all under Heaven.' (Broken Sword)

What was your reaction to the King's plan to create one empire out of divided China? How did you feel about the process he was using to achieve this goal? Why do you think Broken Sword had become persuaded that this was right? How does this compare with God's plan to restore peace to his kingdom?

12. 'Swordsmanship's first achievement is the unity of man and sword. Once this unity is attained, even a blade of grass can be a weapon. The second achievement is when the sword exists in one's heart when absent from one's hand. One can strike an enemy at a hundred paces, even with bare hands. Swordsmanship's ultimate achievement is the absence of the sword in both hand and heart. The swordsman is at peace with the rest of the world. He vows not to kill and to bring peace to mankind.' (King of Qin)

'A dead man asks you to remember the highest ideal of the warrior ... that he lay down his sword.' (Nameless' final words)

Do you think *Hero* glorifies violence, or condemns it? Why? What biblical principles do you think are most appropriate to bring into a discussion of this point?

13. Compare Nameless' quote from the previous question with Jesus' words in Matthew 5:38–42. What are the parallels between the two? What are the differences?

14. The Chinese government has to give its approval to all films made in China, and, unusually, gave Yimou Zhang permission to film in the Forbidden City. To what extent do you agree with suggestions that *Hero* is propaganda for the totalitarian Chinese government? Do these allegations change your feelings about the film?

15. 'People give up their lives for many reasons. For friendship, for love, for an ideal. And people kill for the same reasons . . .' (title cards)

    The assassins and Nameless were all willing both to kill and to sacrifice themselves for their cause. Why do you think they were willing to go to such lengths? How does this compare with what the early Christians were prepared to face in spreading the gospel (see 2 Corinthians 11:16–33)?

Notes

[1] Quoted in Daniel Eagan, 'Martial Artist: China's Zhang Yimou Turns to Action Genre' in *Film Journal International*, 1 September 2004 – www.filmjournal.com/filmjournal/filmmakers/article_display.jsp?vnu_content_id=1000692658

[2] Damon Wise, 'Big Trouble in Little China', *Empire*, Issue 184 (October 2004), p. 92

The danger can be that the road is really narrow. Not everyone can walk it, and if you don't live up to biblical standards, you risk being left behind, alone and alienated. It's hard enough being a teenager without having to make the path so difficult with no room for mistakes. God knows I made plenty.

Brian Dannelly

7. *Not the End of the World* – Study Guide

Tony Watkins

Book Title: *Not the End of the World*
Author: Geraldine McCaughrean
Publisher: Oxford University Press
Date of publication: 7 October 2004

Key Issues

Tolerance, God, families, disaster, hospitality, compassion, kindness

Summary

Noah and his sons have built the ark, vast numbers of familiar and unfamiliar animals have arrived, and now the family are making final preparations. The Flood is imminent. The neighbours still haven't a clue what this fanatical, stand-offish, and apparently crazy family are up to. They are bewildered and troubled by the exotic or fierce animals which have arrived from nowhere. They have not the slightest inkling about what is soon to befall them – and nobody in Noah's family is going to let them in on the secret.

The rain begins. Soon they will be safe within the ark while everything else gets swept away. Shem is delighted – in his mind a great new future is in store with him at the very centre. Ham seems untroubled by it. But youngest brother Japheth, a sensitive 12-year-old, is much less certain. All he can think about is the destruction. All those people; all those animals; his best friend Abram. On the last night before the ark is afloat, the brothers bundle young Zillah out of her family's tent and take her onto the great vessel. It was Ham's wife Sarai's suggestion: the older brothers have wives but Japheth will also need a wife in the new world, and who better than her best friend Zillah? Japheth can't even remember who Zillah is until they get her on board, and he feels much too young to think about being married anyway.

As the waters rise, the realities of the cataclysm sink in. The ark pitches violently, and in the bowels of the ship the animals are terrified as they are flung around in the dark, separated from their natural environments and shut up in a dark box full of terrifying, tempting, or just alien smells. All around the ship is the flotsam and jetsam of a world which is being swept away: cooking pots, fences, livestock. And people. People drowning; people clinging for dear life on to driftwood; people clinging to the ark begging for rescue. But instead of pulling survivors aboard, Shem and Ham patrol the decks 'wielding lengths of timber – slashing and fending off' (p. 5). Shem's wife Bashemath rejoices in the purging of the world from all these wicked people. Sarai and Zillah are retching with sickness and grief. Japheth hides in the aviaries, fingers in his ears, sobbing. Noah sits, deep in prayer, while his wife urges their daughter Timna to keep to her place and do as her father told her. Their voyage has begun.

Background

Geraldine McCaughrean is the only author to have won the Whitbread Children's Award three times – first in 1987 for *A Little Lower Than the Angels*, then in 1994 for *Gold Dust*, and then in 2005 for *Not the End of the World*. The judges said:

> 'With stunning imaginative force, rank physicality and luminous writing, this unsentimental book makes the old story utterly new, and engages with crucial matters – tolerance and the dangers of fundamentalism.'[1]

Reviewer Diane Samuels says that *Not the End of the World*:

> 'is an intriguing, brave and flawed book. Its grand design seems to be to question patriarchal values and fundamentalist attitudes by revealing the underbelly of human experience, located especially in the women. Here, the God of the Old Testament is harsh. Timna must escape this world view and the men who hold sway over her in order to flourish in a more humanistic, compassionate tradition, and to offer the reader hope for the future.'[2]

Geraldine McCaughrean has had nearly 140 books published, including novels, retellings of great myths, and several collections of stories. While writing *Not the End of the World* she suffered from writer's block for the first time. Having already lost what she had written when a power surge hit her computer, and then having lost the contents of her notebook when it got rained on, she found herself unable to continue the story: 'I thought [writer's block] was a thing only used by prats as an excuse for not writing: and then it hit me; I physically could not put pen to paper.'[3] Finally she set a quota of words to write each day until she got through it.

McCaughrean is the youngest of three children. She says:

> 'My brother and sister were immensely clever, which didn't do my self-esteem much good because I wasn't. As my sister comfortingly put it once: "Don't worry, the third one's always stupid."'

Writing in *The Guardian*, Dina Rabinovitch reflects on Geraldine McCaughrean's shyness and says:

> 'Low self-esteem is a part of her story, and reflected in her heroines, who are usually little-regarded, like the daughter she invents for Noah.'[4]

Geraldine initially trained to be a teacher, but didn't enjoy it at all ('I wept my way through teaching practice'), so she went to work for a publishing company. She says she is driven to write by:

> 'the same thing that drove me as a child: the desire to escape the mundane and unsatisfactory here and now and go somewhere else and be someone else for a while, living out an adventure. I hope that my books provide that same escape route for the reader – a brief excursion into a different, colourful world made in the knowledge of a safe return at the end.'[5]

In March 2005, McCaughrean won an international competition to write a sequel to J. M. Barrie's *Peter Pan*.

Questions for Discussion

1. What were your feelings about the Flood story before reading *Not the End of the World?* What emotions did the book stir up in you? Did you find it had a particular resonance because of the South East Asian tsunami in December 2004?

2. Why do you think Geraldine McCaughrean invented Noah's daughter Timna and made her voice the primary one in the book? How would you describe Timna?

3. 'God wept and his tears have drowned the world. But first he reached out and plucked me and my family to safety. So why can't I lift up my heart in praise? I must be so ungrateful, so thankless.' (p. 10)
   How does Timna feel about God?

4. 'Father knows best. It's not for us women to talk about the ways of God.' (Timna's mother, p.19)
   Would it be fair to describe *Not the End of the World* as a feminist version of the Flood story? Why/why not?

5. With which character do you most identify? Why? To what extent do you feel that Geraldine McCaughrean has made it impossible to sympathise with some of the characters?

6. 'Me, I'm in harmony with the Lord's way of thinking. I have every sympathy with Him. I saw what scum had risen to the surface of the world ... how it had to be skimmed off. The world had to be cleansed. This way it will be clean again in time for my boy to be born. Our son. *My* son. ... Do you

realise, I'm bearing the new Adam! King of the new world!' (Bashemath, p. 14)

How would you describe Shem and Bashemath? Why do you think McCaughrean has made them so egotistical? To what extent are they right (see Genesis 6:5–7)?

7. 'I could hear Shem grunting as he swung back his stick, and the crack as it landed in a face or haunch or back.' (Timna, p. 5)

Is there any justification for the way Shem and Ham acted towards survivors of the Flood? How do you feel about the way Shem acted towards his family, and to Bashemath in particular?

8. '"God will reach out His hand," said father, patting my head, then he squatted down to pray, covering his face with his hands, like a man washing.' (p. 58)

'"I regret to say: she must die," says my father sadly. . . . Father is grief-stricken, of course, but that won't do me any good. Father has been sacrificing his own happiness all life long to please God. Self-sacrifice gets to be a habit. A happiness in itself, almost. Father won't change the habit of a lifetime just to save me.' (p. 147, 149)

How is Noah portrayed in *Not the End of the World*? To what extent is the book on his side? What impression of Noah do you get from the biblical account of the Flood in Genesis 6–9?

9. What kind of person is Japheth? How does he change during the course of the story? What do you think about his relationship with Zillah and with the rest of his family?

10. Who would you say is the hero/heroine of the book? Why? What do you think Geraldine McCaughrean is suggesting by this?

11. Were you surprised by Noah's wife (especially pages 152–159)? If so, in what ways?

12. 'Father's sincere ... And I'm going to believe him! Not because I'm certain – I have no idea if he heard God right! But that's what sons *do!* It's one of the rules. I understand rules. I'm going to take his word for it that God's on his side. Otherwise ...' (Japheth, p. 163)
    Why do you think Japheth says this?

13. 'How much worse it would be if the Flood was NOT God's doing; if it was just too big for Him to handle – a natural disaster bigger than even He could avert. Much worse: what if The Wave caught *Him* unawares and knocked Him down and left Him floundering, out of His depth? But the constellations are still up there, pointing the way west, aren't they? The constellations didn't drown, did they? And surely God is bigger than them! However crotchety, however drunk, however harassed by His dog, or by the Unrighteous, or by carpenters who get His instructions wrong, surely God is bigger than the pictures He chalked on the night sky?' (Timna, p. 166).
    To what extent do you agree with her? How does this perspective help you to think about natural disasters, such as the South East Asian tsunami? What other biblical perspectives do we need to bring into our thinking about such things (see for example Genesis 3:17; Romans 8:20–22; Psalm 135:6; Isaiah 30:18; Luke 13:1–5)?

14. Timna: 'Father's a wonderful man. Full of righteousness. Strong in the Lord. It's just that he has to do what God tells him.'
    Kittim: 'And God would tell him to throw me overboard? ... God's mad too, then.' (p. 74)
    Timna: 'A great resentment boiled up inside me against Shem and Ham and Bashemath and Sarai and mother – even against father, for being so *certain*. For having no questions at all, at all, at all in their tidy, holy minds.' (p. 143)

    How is intolerance portrayed in *Not the End of the World*? What does Geraldine McCaughrean see as the alternative? To what extent do you agree with her? What other values come across as important in the book?

15. What do you think she is suggesting about faith in God? Why do most of the animals affirm that the God of their species is good, and the final sentence of the book state that 'the Finch God is very, very good' (p. 174) (see Isaiah 55:6–13; Jeremiah 10:1–16; Romans 11:33–36)?

16. To what extent do you agree with the comment that, 'Hospitality is a quirk of the human breed. Hard to suppress. Like violence and lust.' (p. 174)? How does this comment fit the picture of human beings we get from Genesis 1–3 – made in God's image yet rebels against him?

17. How do you think Geraldine McCaughrean wants her readers to think about God, religion and other people after reading *Not the End of the World*?

Notes

[1] *The Independent*, 6 January 2005 – enjoyment.independent.co.uk/books/news/story.jsp?story=598158
[2] *The Guardian*, 18 December 2004 – books.guardian.co.uk/reviews/childrenandteens/0,6121,1376223,00.html
[3] Dina Rabinovitch, 'Author of the month: Geraldine McCaughrean' in *The Guardian*, 19 January 2005 – books.guardian.co.uk/departments/childrenandteens/story/0,6000,1393703,00.html
[4] Dina Rabinovitch, 'Author of the month: Geraldine McCaughrean'
[5] Judith Ridge, 'Interview with Geraldine McCaughrean' – www.misrule.com.au/mccaughrean2.html

It is different, yeah, it's a different morality. Get used to it or go home.

The Doctor in *Doctor Who*

8. *Doctor Who* – Study Guide

Tony Watkins

Programme Title: *Doctor Who*
Screenplay by: Russell T. Davies (with Mark Gatiss, Robert Shearman, Paul Cornell and Steve Moffat)
Producer: Phil Collinson
Executive Producers: Russell T. Davies, Julie Gardner and Mal Young
Starring: Christopher Eccleston, Billie Piper
Production Company: BBC Wales
Broadcaster: BBC1
First Broadcast: 26 March 2005 (original series first broadcast: 23 November 1963)
DVD Release Dates: 16 May 2005 (episodes 1–3); 13 June 2005 (episodes 4–7); August 2005 (episodes 8–10); September 2005 (episodes 11–13); 21 November 2005 (Complete Season 1 boxset)

Note: Due to publication schedules, this book had to be completed before the 2005 series of *Doctor Who* was finished. This study guide is therefore based only on the first few episodes.

Key Issues

Humanity, death, morality, tolerance, fear, hope

Summary

Nineteen-year-old Rose Tyler is almost the last to leave the High Street clothing store in which she works. Before leaving she has an errand to run down to the basement of the building. She fails to find the man she's looking for, but is spooked by some shop dummies which start to move. At first she thinks someone is playing tricks, but she begins to feel they mean her harm. Just as things turn nasty, a hand pulls her to safety. The Doctor is back on earth. He helps her escape from an ever-increasing number of malevolent mannequins, but she ends up going home with an arm from one of them. The Doctor later tracks the arm to her flat where it comes to life and attacks them.

Rose tags along as the Doctor tries to track down an old foe, the Nestene Consciousness – the mind which animates and controls plastic objects including the mannequins, otherwise known as the Autons. The Doctor seems to find Rose quite a special human being in that she seems not to be fazed by the extraordinary things he tells her, she doesn't panic (unlike many previous companions!), and she is also able to think for herself. Not only can she see what the Doctor overlooks, but her quick thinking and fearless action save the day.

After transporting Rose and her boyfriend Mickey away from danger, the Doctor invites Rose to join him on his travels. At first she refuses, but when the TARDIS reappears just moments after leaving, she changes her mind without any hesitation. Travelling through time and space is quite a novelty, and the Doctor first takes Rose five billion years into the future to gather with a diverse group of aliens to watch the end of the earth as it is absorbed by the sun. After the excitement of the far future, they go back in time to Cardiff in 1869. They meet Charles Dickens and encounter ghostly emanations from the mouths of reanimated corpses. The Doctor is sure it's alien activity, and before long he is attempting to rescue the Gelth from their fate, only to discover they really have sinister motives.

Then it's back to London so that Rose can see her mother and Mickey. But while they talk, an alien spaceship clips Big Ben and crashes into the Thames. Its occupants, the Slitheen, are intent on provoking nuclear warfare so that they can sell lumps of the irradiated planet off to other aliens who need energy at knock-down prices. Once again, it's down to the Doctor to save the planet – helped by Rose and Mickey. Later, a distress call intercepted by the TARDIS takes them deep underground in the near future – into billionaire Henry van Statten's secret collection of alien relics where they find an old enemy, the last of the Daleks. Rose's pity for it leads to its escape, but also brings about something of an emotional revolution for the exterminator, and she finds herself standing between it and the Doctor who is bent on its final destruction.

Time travel enables Rose to meet the father she never knew, but her interference in the course of history has a catastrophic effect. The Doctor begins to wonder if she isn't really just as stupid as other humans after all. A heady mix of thrills and dangers – including an encounter with another time traveller, Captain Jack, in the London Blitz – are among the treats still in store for

Rose, not to mention the surprise she'll get when the Doctor regenerates into a new body.

Background

Doctor Who was first broadcast by the BBC on 23 November 1963 with William Hartnell as 'the Doctor' (not 'Doctor Who' – the series title is really a question, not the main character's name). Since then the Doctor has ranged through time and space, sorting out problematic aliens. The Doctor is, of course, an alien himself – he may look human (a casual inspection doesn't reveal that he has two hearts) but he is a Time Lord from Gallifrey. His famous TARDIS (the name comes from Time And Relative Dimensions In Space) should take on an external appearance to suit whatever environment he finds himself in, but a malfunction in the 'chameleon circuit' left it in the form of a 1950s police telephone box. From time to time, the Doctor undergoes a process of regeneration which gives him a new external form and some differences in personality. This is a useful device for allowing a series of actors to play the part over the years – Christopher Eccleston is the ninth.[1]

During the mid-1980s the audience figures dropped substantially and the BBC rested the show for a year and a half from early 1985 until September 1986. Three years later, *Doctor Who* was dropped entirely from the schedules, notwithstanding the howls of protest from the army of fans. The Doctor made a brief reappearance in 1996 for a TV movie, but it was not until September 2003 that the BBC finally agreed to commission a new series. The new material is mostly written by Russell T. Davies who is best known for his controversial series

Queer as Folk and the two-part drama *The Second Coming* (also starring Christopher Eccleston) which ended with the final death of God. The viewing figures for the first episode of *Doctor Who* in March 2005 were so good that the BBC immediately commissioned a Christmas Special and a second series. Christopher Eccleston declined to continue into the second series, though Billie Piper will carry on playing Rose. The tenth Doctor is to be Scottish actor David Tennant, who has recently starred in *Casanova* (also written by Russell T. Davies and broadcast by the BBC).

For more information, see the BBC's *Doctor Who* website www.bbc.co.uk/doctorwho and a tie-in site, www.whoisdoctorwho.co.uk.

Questions for Discussion

1. What do you think the appeal of *Doctor Who* is? Why do you think so many fans stayed loyal to the show during the sixteen years since it was last shown regularly on British television? Do you think they will be satisfied by the new series?

2. What do you personally most enjoy about *Doctor Who?* Are there any aspects you do not like?

3. 'The Doctor is a legend woven throughout history. When disaster comes, he's there. He brings a storm in his wake and he has one constant companion . . . death.' (Clive in episode 1, 'Rose')

    'If he's singled you out, if the Doctor's making house calls, then God help you.' (Clive in episode 1, 'Rose').

    Doctor Who has always been known as a programme to make children hide behind the sofa. Has that ever been your experience, or the experience of any children you know? What makes it scary? Do you think it's good for children to encounter programmes which scare them? Why/why not?

4. Which (if any) of the earlier Doctors do you remember? Which do you prefer most? Why?

5. What do you think are the Doctor's greatest strengths and greatest weaknesses?

6. How would you describe the character of the Doctor as played by Christopher Eccleston? How does he compare to previous Doctors in terms of his personality?

7. How would you describe Rose Tyler's character? In what ways is she similar to/different from previous companions?

8. 'He's not my boyfriend, Mickey, he's better than that. He's much more important.' (Rose in episode 4, 'Aliens of London')

    'I could save the world but lose you.' (The Doctor in episode 5, 'World War Three')

    What is the relationship between the Doctor and Rose like? How is it developing?

9. What would you identify as the key themes of *Doctor Who*? Do you think the treatment of these themes is different from the way they were handled in earlier series? Why/why not?

10. 'So maybe this is it: first contact, the day mankind officially comes into contact with an alien race. I'm not interfering 'cause you've got to handle this on your own. That's when the human race finally

grows up. This morning you were tiny and small and made of clay, now you can expand!' (The Doctor in episode 4, 'Aliens of London')

'You lot, you spend all your time thinking about dying. Like you're going to get killed by eggs, or beef, or global warming or asteroids. But you never take time to imagine the impossible – that maybe you survive.' (The Doctor in episode 2, 'The End of the World')

Is *Doctor Who* essentially optimistic or pessimistic about human nature? What does it mean to be a human being according to *Doctor Who*? How does this view compare to the biblical view (see Genesis 5:1–2; Psalm 8; Romans 1:18–25)?

11. 'Everything has its time, and everything dies.' (The Doctor in episode 2, 'The End of the World')

    What is the Doctor's perspective on death? How does it differ from Rose's view? How do their views compare with your own perspective? What is a biblical view of death? See, for example, Ecclesiastes 3:18–21; 12:7; Hebrews 9:27; 1 Corinthians 15:21–28, 42–56.

12. Would you be regenerated if you could be? Why/why not? What would you want the new you to be like? How does the idea of regeneration compare with the Christian belief in resurrection to eternal life of those who have put their trust in Jesus Christ? See, for example, John 5:24–29; 1 Corinthians 15:35–54.

13. 'Guests are reminded that Platform One forbids the use of weapons, teleportation and religion.' (announcement in episode 2, 'The End of the World')

What would you say is the view of *Doctor Who* towards spiritual realities?

14. Can you identify the moral values of *Doctor Who?* Which would you endorse? Which wouldn't you endorse? Why?

15. Alan McKee wrote in *Intensities: The Journal of Cult Media*[2] that, '*Doctor Who* includes the celebration of tolerance, peaceful coexistence and the celebration of difference.'

    Can you think of examples which would back up this comment? In what ways is the Doctor tolerant?

16. Are there limits to tolerance, peaceful coexistence and the celebration of difference? If so, what are they? How do you think the Doctor would answer that question? What do Romans 12:9–21, 2 Corinthians 10:3–5 and Ephesians 5:1–14 suggest about tolerance and its limits? What other passages are relevant?

17. Charles Dickens: 'Can it be that I have the world entirely wrong?'
    The Doctor: 'You're not wrong, there's just more to learn.' (Episode 3, 'The Unquiet Dead')

    What do you think the Doctor means by his reply? What is the relationship between tolerance and truth within *Doctor Who?* Do you agree with *Doctor Who's* perspective on tolerance? Why/why not?

Notes

[1] After William Hartnell and before Christopher Eccleston came Patrick Troughton (1966–1969), Jon Pertwee (1970–

1974), Tom Baker (1974–1981), Peter Davison (1982–1984), Colin Baker (1984–1986), Sylvester McCoy (1987–1989) and Paul McGann (1996 TV movie only). Peter Cushing also played the role in two films in the 1960s, but his Doctor is not considered to be part of the official canon.

[2] Alan McKee, 'Which is the best Doctor Who story? A case study in value judgements outside the academy', *Intensities: The Journal of Cult Media* –
www.cult-media.com/issue1/Amckee.htm

I only draw the line of what's unacceptable according to my personal taste, not by what other people judge as acceptable. I do things that suit me and feel right.

Marilyn Manson

9. Definitely Maybe – the Philosophy of David Hume

Peter S. Williams

> 'Hume ... developed to its logical conclusion the empirical philosophy of Locke and Berkeley, and by making it self-consistent made it incredible.'
>
> (Bertrand Russell)[1]

David Hume (1711–1776) is Scotland's most famous philosopher. He considered a career in law, but had, 'an insurmountable aversion to everything but the pursuits of philosophy and general learning.'[2] Many scholars consider the *Treatise of Human Nature* (1739–1740) to be Hume's most important work and one of the most important books in the history of philosophy. At the time, Hume lamented that the volume, 'fell dead-born from the press', and he reworked some of the material into the more popular *An Enquiry Concerning Human Understanding*. Hume remains an influential philosophical voice today, primarily because many contemporary atheists embrace his scepticism and empiricism.

Sceptical About Metaphysics – There is No Fork

In the conclusion of his *Enquiry*, Hume summarised the basis of his scepticism:

> 'When we run over libraries, persuaded of these principles, what havoc must we make? If we take in hand any volume; of divinity or school metaphysics, for instance; let us ask, Does it contain any abstract reasoning concerning quantity or number? No. Does it contain any experimental reasoning concerning matters of fact or existence? No. Commit it to the flames: For it can contain nothing but sophistry and illusion.'[3]

In other words, if something has no mathematical or scientific basis it is worthless – an approach to knowledge called *empiricism*. Hume's test for the worth of an idea is known as 'Hume's Fork' and is a grand example of the pot calling the kettle black. This becomes obvious if we ask whether Hume's Fork contains any 'abstract reasoning concerning number' or any 'experimental reasoning concerning existence'? The answer, in both cases, is 'No'. To be consistent, Hume would have to commit his own conclusion to the flames! This is a self-destructive philosophy:

> 'Hume's contention that all meaningful statements are either a relation of ideas or else about matters of fact is itself neither of these. Hence, on its own grounds it would be meaningless.'[4]

Hume's empiricism led him to be sceptical about metaphysics, which we may define as: 'philosophical inquiry that does *not* confine itself to abstract reasoning concerning quantity or number and experimental reasoning concerning matters of fact or existence.' Metaphysics includes the fields of ethics (the study of moral value) and aesthetics (the study of beauty), as well as philosophical thinking about the existence of God, etc. Hume believed that it is impossible to find objectively true answers to metaphysical questions. Hence he thought it impossible to find objectively true answers to questions about what is right or wrong, beautiful or ugly. According to Hume's Fork, any attempt to give an objective answer to metaphysical questions, including questions about value, must, 'contain nothing but sophistry and illusion'. It follows that metaphysical questions can only have answers that are *subjective* or *relative* in nature, the kind of answer where 'what's true *for you* may not be true *for me*'.

Sceptical About Beauty

For example, Hume advocated a subjective view of beauty, writing that:

> 'All sentiment is right; because sentiment has a reference to nothing beyond itself, and is always right, whenever a man is conscious of it. But all determinations of the understanding are not right; because they have a reference to something beyond themselves, to wit, a real matter of fact; and are not always conformable to that standard ... Beauty is no quality in things themselves: it exists merely in the mind which contemplates them; and each mind perceives a different beauty.'[5]

In other words, any feelings about beauty are true for the person who experiences them because they are entirely a product of the mind. But thinking about 'facts' in the real world is a different matter – it is possible to be wrong about such things; it's an objective issue. Hume subjectively defined beauty as, 'nothing but a form which produces pleasure'.[6] Hence, if masochistic acts produce in me a feeling of pleasure, then masochism is 'beautiful', *for me*. Beauty depends upon personal pleasure, and is therefore relative to the subject. No aesthetic judgements can be false, because no one can be mistaken about their own subjective reactions: 'Sublimity [i.e. beauty] does not reside in any of the things of nature, but only in our own mind.'[7] As C. S. Lewis explained, on this basis:

> 'the world of facts, without one trace of value, and the world of feelings, without one trace of truth or falsehood, justice or injustice, confront each other, and no rapprochement is possible.'[8]

Hume's view puts the cart before the horse. In fact we experience aesthetic value, like moral value, as a reality beyond ourselves: 'Beauty belongs, *prima facie*, to things. It is not emotions which are beautiful but that which arouses them.'[9]

Sceptical About Causality

As an empiricist, Hume believed that all knowledge of matters of fact comes via the five senses. Hume said the world makes 'impressions' upon us through our senses that form the basis of 'ideas' (faint copies of impressions) in our minds. Hume thought that these ideas could only be related to each other by mental custom or habit, and that such relationships of ideas do not necessarily represent the way things are in the real world. That is, we make all kinds of connections between ideas in our minds, but that might have no connection to the way things are. Indeed, Hume argued that causation, the principle of cause and effect (e.g. one billiard ball's *causing* another to move by hitting it), is *nothing but* 'a determination of the mind'.

Hume did not deny the principle of causality that 'from nothing, nothing comes'. He admitted it would be absurd to say that things (like forks) pop into existence without a cause. But he denied that there is any way to *establish* this principle of causality – he denied that it could be proved. However:

> 'the very denial of causal necessity implies some kind of causal necessity in the denial. For unless there is a necessary ground (or cause) for the denial, then the denial does not necessarily stand. And if there is a necessary ground or cause for the denial, then the denial is self-defeating . . .'[10]

As C. S. Lewis observed, naturalism (believing only in physical reality, denying the supernatural) gives us no reason to think of our belief in the principle of cause and effect as anything but 'a fact about us' (i.e. all we can say is that this is something we happen to believe) because this belief 'can be trusted only if quite a different Metaphysic is true'.[11] That is: 'If the deepest thing in reality . . . is a thing in some degree like ourselves . . . then indeed our conviction can be trusted.'[12] If a necessary and reliable personal being created the universe, then it is rational to expect the universe to be orderly. Indeed, science was born out of belief in a rational God who had made a rational cosmos and humans with rational minds fitted to understanding their environment.[13]

Sceptical About The Self

Hume denied the common sense distinction between a person and the various features of that person's mental life. He argued that when you introspect you notice a bunch of thoughts, feeling and perceptions, but you don't perceive anything you could call 'the self'. So far as we can tell, said Hume, there is nothing to 'the self' over and above a 'bundle' of mental states. For Hume, perceptions *exist*, but they do not *belong to* anyone. This makes the question of personal identity over time problematical. Can I be *one and the same person as woke up this morning* if the thoughts and feelings that existed then don't exist now? J. P. Moreland and William Lane Craig object:

> 'If we were not already aware of ourselves, how would we know which stream of consciousness or which body to investigate in order to confirm or rule out an awareness of my "I"? Introspection and knowledge of one's body and mental life presupposes awareness of the "I".'[14]

Hume admitted that he was dissatisfied with his account of the self, but he never returned to the issue.

Sceptical About Freedom

Hume distinguished between two meanings of 'free will'. The first, which he called *liberty of difference*, is the common meaning of free will: the ability to make choices that are not the necessary effect of prior causes. The second, which he called *liberty of spontaneity*, means only that someone's actions are not forcibly constrained or hindered. On the assumption that we observe in human affairs 'the same uniformity and regular operation of natural principles'[15] found in the physical world, Hume argued that *there is no liberty of difference*. Our actions are the necessary effects of prior causes (and those causes the effects of further prior causes, etc.). However, we can still be described as 'free', *in the sense of having liberty of spontaneity*, if our actions are not the effect of *outside* causes forcing or preventing us doing what the series of causes that ended up *inside* us caused us to attempt to do. If that happens – for example, if I try to go for a walk (as a result of an internal series of cause and effect) but am prevented from doing so by being in prison – then I lack liberty of spontaneity.

Does liberty of spontaneity have any significance without liberty of difference? What does it matter that my 'decision' to go for a walk is frustrated if my 'decision' is just the result of a chain of causes over which I have no control, no liberty of difference? Hume reduces all talk of, 'I have decided to do something' to talk of, 'I have been caused to do something'. Many philosophers would argue that such a reduction is contradicted by the reality of moral accountability – if I was *caused* to steal, can I be *morally responsible* for stealing? It is also contradicted by the reality of rationality – if I am *caused* to arrive at a conclusion *because of the way the natural world works*, can I have arrived at that conclusion *because there was good reason to do so*?[16]

Sceptical About Arguments for God

According to Isaiah Berlin, Hume died, 'as he had lived, an atheist . . .'[17] However, Hume expert (and founder of the Hume Society) Nicholas Capaldi states that:

'In none of his writings does Hume say or imply that he does not accept the existence of God. On the contrary, Hume says in several places that he accepts the existence of God.'[18]

What Hume *did* reject was the traditional formulations of a number of arguments for God. This is hardly surprising given his scepticism about metaphysics. Hume's objections to the design argument (the universe is like a manufactured object and so probably has an analogous, intelligent cause) are well known. But these objections had the effect of limiting rather than eliminating the conclusion of the argument. (On the one hand, inferences to design are examples of experimental reasoning, often involving consideration of probabilities. On the other hand, arguments about the specific nature of a designer, or the number of designers, are metaphysical.)

For example, Hume objected: 'A great number of men join in building a house or a ship, in rearing a city, in framing a commonwealth, why may not several deities combine in framing a world?'[19] Belief in design is certainly compatible with belief in more than one designer. However, as Stephen T. Davis asks, 'If there is more than one designer, exactly how many are there? And why do they cooperate? Those questions do not need to be asked if there is but one designer.'[20] Moreover, we live in a *uni*verse of 'diversity in unity'. Richard Swinburne notes:

'If there were more than one deity responsible for the order of the universe, we should expect to see characteristic marks of the handiwork of different deities in different parts of the universe, just as we see different workmanship in the different houses of a city.'[21]

But as Hume wrote in his *Natural History of Religion* (1757):

> 'The whole frame of nature bespeaks an intelligent author; and no rational enquirer can, after serious reflection, suspend his belief a moment with regard to the primary principles of genuine Theism . . . All things of the universe are evidently of a piece. Every thing is adjusted to every thing. One design prevails throughout the whole. And this uniformity leads the mind to acknowledge one author.'[22]

Philosophers John Perry and Michael Bratman conclude:

> 'The mature Hume was a theist, albeit of a vague and weak-kneed sort. He seems to have been convinced by the argument from design of the proposition that, "The cause or causes of order in the universe probably bear some remote analogy to human intelligence." But he was also convinced that the argument does not permit this undefined intelligence to be given further shape or specificity . . .'[23]

Hume's most famous modern day philosophical disciple, Professor Antony Flew, recently moved from atheism to theism 'of a vague and weak-kneed sort' on the basis of the design argument as advanced by the intelligent design movement.[24] It is interesting to note that, like Hume, intelligent design theorists draw a distinction between scientific inferences from nature to intelligent design, and metaphysical discussions aimed at giving further shape to the designing intelligence in question.[25] Hume's critique of the design argument (although many scholars think it over-rated[26]) is a helpful corrective to any natural theology that seeks to rest the case for God on any one argument rather than upon an accumulation of arguments. As Hume says, 'When we infer any particular cause for an effect we must proportion the one to the other, and can never be allowed to ascribe to any cause any qualities, but what are exactly sufficient to produce the effect.'[27]

Sceptical About Miracles

In his *Enquiry*, Hume introduced an influential argument against the credibility of belief in miracles: 'I flatter myself that I have discovered an argument ... which, if just, will, with the wise and learned, be an everlasting check to all kinds of superstitious delusion, and consequently will be useful as long as the world endures.'[28] In Hume's own words:

1) 'A miracle is a violation of the laws of nature'
2) 'Firm and unalterable experience has established these laws'
3) 'A wise man proportions his belief to the evidence'
4) Therefore: 'the proof against miracles ... is as entire as any argument from experience can possibly be imagined.'[29]

According to the 'hard' interpretation of this argument (adopted by nineteenth century liberal theologian David Strauss), Hume is arguing that:

1) Miracles, by definition, are a violation of natural law

2) Natural laws are unalterably uniform

3) Therefore, miracles cannot occur.

Hume appears to be using this 'hard' argument when he says, 'it is a miracle that a dead man should come to life, because that has never been observed in any age or century.'[30] However, this 'hard' argument begs the question against miracles by *defining* miracles as unobserved and impossible events:

> 'We must agree with Hume that if there is absolutely "uniform experience" against miracles, if in other words they have never happened, why then they never have. Unfortunately we know the experience against them to be uniform only if we know that all reports of them are false. And we can know all the reports to be false only if we know already that miracles have never occurred. In fact, we are arguing in a circle.'[31]

C. S. Lewis pointed out that belief in God, which renders belief in the uniformity of nature more than a mere 'determination of the mind', also renders miracles possible:

> 'Theology says to you in effect, "Admit God and with Him the risk of a few miracles, and I in return will ratify your faith in uniformity as regards the overwhelming majority of events." The philosophy which forbids you to make uniformity absolute is also the philosophy which offers you solid grounds for believing it to be general ... The alternative is really much worse. Try to make Nature absolute and you find that her uniformity is not even probable. You get the deadlock, as in Hume.'[32]

Hume's argument can also be interpreted as arguing, 'not for the impossibility of miracles but for the *incredibility* of accepting miracles.'[33] This 'soft' version of Hume's argument runs as follows:

1) A miracle is by definition a rare occurrence
2) A natural law is by definition a description of a regular occurrence
3) The evidence for the regular is always greater than the evidence for the rare
4) A wise man always bases his belief on the greater evidence
5) Therefore, a wise man should never believe a miracle has happened.

Norman Geisler comments that on this 'soft' interpretation of the argument:

> 'the rationality of belief in miracles is eliminated, since by the very nature of the case no thoughtful person should ever hold that a miracle has indeed occurred.'[34]

However, as John Earman argues:

> 'An epistemology [theory of knowledge] that does not allow for the possibility that evidence, whether from eyewitness testimony or from other source, can establish the credibility of a UFO landing, a walking on water, or a resurrection is inadequate.'[35]

Hume's argument proves too much. One might expect an empiricist to argue that it is irrational to believe in a miracle without *sufficient* evidence (a position that leaves open the possibility of being rationally convinced that a miracle has happened), but Hume argues that the evidence for a miracle can *never* be sufficient for rational belief *even if a miracle has happened*. Even if Jesus *did* rise from the dead, and you were one of the people who *actually* met and talked with him afterwards, Hume says that you ought not to believe it!

Hume says we should always believe what is most probable. But as Geisler observes:

> 'On these grounds ... we should never believe we have been dealt a perfect bridge hand (though this has happened) since the odds against it are 1,635,013,559,600 to 1!'[36]

Sometimes the *probability* of an event based on past observation is low, but the *evidence* for the event is very good based on current observation and/or reliable testimony:

> 'if a number of independent probabilities converge upon an alleged miraculous event, and alternative naturalistic explanations are inadequate to explain the data ... it becomes entirely reasonable to believe that this miraculous event has occurred.'[37]

Geisler concludes:

> 'Hume's argument confuses *quantity* of evidence with the *quality* of evidence ... The wise do not *legislate* in advance that miracles cannot be believed to have happened; rather, they *look* at the evidence to see if God has indeed acted in history.'[38]

By such an investigation one may hope to bring some specific content to Hume's 'weak-kneed' acknowledgement of a cosmic designer.

Notes

[1] Bertrand Russell, *A History of Western Philosophy* (Allen and Unwin, 1946), p. 658
[2] David Hume, www.wikipedia.org/wiki/David_Hume
[3] David Hume, *Enquiry Concerning Human Understanding*, 12.3
[4] Norman L. Geisler, *Christian Apologetics* (Baker, 1996), p. 22
[5] David Hume, *On the Standard of Taste*
[6] David Hume, *A Treatise of Human Nature*
[7] David Hume, *A Treatise of Human Nature*
[8] C.S. Lewis, *The Abolition of Man* (Fount, 1978), p. 16
[9] C. E. M. Joad, *The Recovery of Belief*, p. 145. I agree with G. E. Moore, who wrote that: 'the beautiful should be *defined* as that of which the admiring contemplation is good in itself … the question whether it is truly beautiful or not, depends upon the *objective* question whether the whole in question is or is not truly good.' (G. E. Moore, *Principia Ethica*, p. 201). See also Peter S. Williams, *I Wish I Could Believe In Meaning: A Response To Nihilism* (Damaris, 2004)
[10] Geisler, *Christian Apologetics*, p. 25
[11] C. S. Lewis, *Miracles*, second edition (Fount, 1996), p. 110
[12] C. S. Lewis, *Miracles*
[13] cf. C. S. Lewis, *Miracles*; Charles Thaxton, 'Christianity and the Scientific Enterprise' – www.leaderu.com/truth/1truth17.html; Alvin Plantinga, 'An Evolutionary Argument Against Naturalism' – hisdefense.org/audio/ap_audio.html
[14] J. P. Moreland and William Lane Craig, *Philosophical Foundations For A Christian Worldview* (IVP, 2003), p. 299
[15] David Hume, quoted in Robert Audi (ed.) *The Cambridge Dictionary of Philosophy*, second edition (Cambridge University Press, 1999), p. 401
[16] cf. Victor Reppert, *C. S. Lewis' Dangerous Idea* (IVP, 2004)
[17] Isaiah Berlin, *The Age of Enlightenment: The 18th Century Philosophers* (Mentor, 1956), p. 163

[18] Nicholas Capaldi, *David Hume* (Hall & Co, 1975), ch. 9; Dave Armstrong, 'Was Skeptical Philosopher David Hume an Atheist?' – ic.net/~erasmus/RAZ515.HTM
[19] David Hume, *Dialogues Concerning Natural Religion*, p. 39
[20] Stephen T. Davis, *God, Reason and Theistic Proofs* (Edinburgh University Press, 1997), p. 103
[21] Richard Swinburne, 'The Argument for Design' in *Contemporary Perspective on Religious Epistemology* (Oxford University Press, 1992), p. 209–210
[22] David Hume, *Natural History of Religion*; Dave Armstrong, 'Was Skeptical Philosopher David Hume an Atheist?' – ic.net/~erasmus/RAZ515.HTM
[23] John Perry and Michael Bratman, *Introduction to Philosophy: Classical and Contemporary Readings* (Oxford University Press, 1998)
[24] See Peter S. Williams, 'A Change of Mind for Antony Flew' – www.arn.org/docs/williams/pw_antonyflew.htm
[25] cf. John G. West, 'Intelligent Design and Creationism Just Aren't the Same' – www.discovery.org/scripts/viewDB/index.php?command=view&program=CSC&id=1329
[26] cf. Richard Swinburne, 'The Argument from Design', in R. Douglas Geivett and Brendan Sweetman (eds.) *Contemporary Perspectives on Religious Epistemology* (Oxford University Press, 1992); Brian Davies, *An Introduction to the Philosophy of Religion*, new edition (Oxford University Press, 1993)
[27] David Hume, *An Enquiry Concerning Human Understanding*, 136
[28] Hume, *An Enquiry Concerning Human Understanding*, 10.1.118
[29] Hume, *An Enquiry Concerning Human Understanding*, 10.1.118
[30] Hume, *An Enquiry Concerning Human Understanding*, 10.1.118
[31] C. S. Lewis, *Miracles*, p. 106
[32] C. S. Lewis, *Miracles*, p. 111
[33] Norman L. Geisler, 'Miracles and the Modern Mind' in

R. Douglas Geivett and Gary R. Habermas (eds.) *In Defence of Miracles* (Apollos, 1997), p. 75

[34] Norman L. Geisler, 'Miracles and the Modern Mind', p. 76

[35] John Earman, *Hume's Abject Failure*, quoted by James Patrick Holding, 'Humean Understanding' – www.tektonics.org/gk/hume01.html

[36] Norman L. Geisler, 'Miracles and the Modern Mind', p. 79

[37] Francis J. Beckwith, 'Theism, Miracles, And the Modern Mind' in Paul Copan and Paul K. Moser (eds.) *The Rationality of Theism* (Routledge, 2003), p. 231

[38] Norman L. Geisler, 'Miracles and the Modern Mind', p. 79, 85.

Background to the Featured Quotes

'If our goal is to achieve ...' (p. xv)

If our goal is to achieve a multi-cultural society that is both free and peaceful, then what we need is not the multiplication of taboos but the expansion of tolerance. The belief in the value of tolerance is not like a belief in Jesus Christ, the prophet Muhammad, Ahura Mazda or, for that matter, the scientific wisdom of Darwin; it's the belief that alone makes it possible for all other beliefs to coexist.

Timothy Garton Ash

Source

The Guardian, 13 January 2005

Background

Timothy Garton Ash is a political columnist and Professor of European Studies in the University of Oxford. He is the author of several books, most recently *Free World:*

Why a Crisis for the West reveals the Opportunity of our Time (Penguin, 2004). He is also a regular contributor to a number of publications, including *The Guardian*, the *New York Times* and the *New York Review of Books*.

'When issues of morality ...' (p. 13)

When issues of morality are very murky, if you don't have a strong definition of right and wrong, you can get lost.

Amanda Donahoe

Source

Interviewed in *The Independent* 13 April 2004

Background

The actress Amanda Donahoe is best known for her roles in the film *Castaway* and the American TV series *LA Law*. She is also the star of ITV's police show *Murder City*.

The interviewer comments on her provocative reputation (she has appeared nude in a number of film roles) and willingness to talk about sex, and how these have obscured 'a very strong sense of morality'.

A longer version of the quote is as follows:

'We are the sum of the choices we make, and if you go into a situation where you know somebody isn't available then any adult must be clear about the consequences; which will be many and immediate, and often bloody painful. I think I have a responsibility, not to anybody else, but to myself, because I think that's important. When issues of morality are very murky, if you don't have a strong definition of right and wrong, you can get lost. I've been in Hollywood, and I saw people get lost.'

'This is England ...' (p. 31)

This is England. You can do whatever you like.

Monica Ali

Source

Brick Lane, Blackswan (2003)

Background

Brick Lane is the story of Nazneen, who was born in Bangladesh but moved to Tower Hamlets, London, in 1985 when she was eighteen for an arranged marriage to Chanu. The novel is a study of Bengali culture in London, and of the clash between the different cultures in Brick Lane and its surrouding area. The book explores the importance of cultural identity, and how misunderstandings about another culture can lead to suspicion and hatred. *Brick Lane* is Monica Ali's first novel.

This quote appears as the very last line of the novel, giving it a real poignancy. Nazneen is taken ice-skating for the first time, and she says that she cannot go ice-skating in a sari. The quote is the response of her friend emphasising the differences between English and Bengali culture, and the relative freedom English people have compared to those in Bangladesh.

'I'm not a practising Catholic ...' (p. 47)

> I'm not a practising Catholic or I wouldn't be living unwed with a woman, and I don't think all poofs are going to hell, and I don't think everyone who's had an abortion is damned. Most of my friends are atheists and I understand atheism, I get it, but I happen to be a theist. I believe in our answerableness to something else.
>
> Martin Freeman, interviewed by Miranda Sawyer

Source

The Observer, 17 April 2005

Background

The actor Martin Freeman first came to widespread public attention in the role of Tim in the BBC comedy *The Office*. Subsequently he has starred in the sitcoms *The Robinsons* and *Hardware* and had supporting roles in the films *Love Actually* and *Shaun of the Dead*. His biggest cinematic role to date has been starring as Arthur Dent in *The Hitchhiker's Guide To The Galaxy*.

Freeman went to a Catholic school, and (as this quote makes clear) still believes in God. Miranda Sawyer follows this quote with the comment: 'Martin's tolerance sits awkwardly with his religion and anger. He's a raging, God-loving, conservative-living liberal.'

'I don't believe . . .' (p. 55)

I don't believe in organised religion, but I treat other people right and use the Ten Commandments . . . well, I'm solid with eight or nine! That other people's wives thing just kills me!

Will Smith

Source

Interviewed in *Q* magazine, April 2005

Background

Will Smith is one of the biggest film actors in the world, having started his career as a rapper (working as 'the Fresh Prince'), moving into TV sitcom (*The Fresh Prince of Bel Air*) and eventually into films such as *Independence Day*, *I, Robot* and *Men In Black*.

This quote, taken from *Q's* 'Cash for Questions' feature (where readers submit questions and get paid £25 for any that are printed), came as Smith reflected on a friend of his who had become 'a devout Christian'. A longer version of the quote is as follows:

'Her first official act was to call me and tell me that I was going to hell. Why? For not dedicating my music and my career and all that stuff to Jesus. I don't believe in organised religion, but I treat other people right and use the Ten Commandments ... well, I'm solid with eight or nine! That other people's wives thing just kills me!'

'Here's to the men ...' (p. 67)

Here's to the men who did what was considered wrong in order to do what they knew was right.
Ben Gates in the film *National Treasure*

Source

National Treasure (Walt Disney, 2004) – certificate PG

Background

National Treasure is a family action-adventure story, centred around one man's life-long search for the missing treasure of the Knights Templar. Benjamin Franklin Gates (Nicolas Cage) inherits the family duty to find and protect the long lost greatest treasure known to man. His search leads him to conclude that the next clue is hidden on the back of the Declaration of Independence. His former colleague Ian (Sean Bean) is, unlike Ben, more interested in the value of the treasure than in the hunt, and sets himself on stealing the Declaration. Ben comes to the realisation that the only way he can safeguard such a precious historic document is to steal it himself.

This line occurs at a cocktail party. Ben is talking to Dr Abigail Chase (Diane Kruger), one of the officials at the National Archive. Dr Chase has previously dismissed Ben's warnings about the threat to the Declaration. Although Dr Chase does not realise it at the time, Ben is justifying his intentions by putting them on a par with those of the Founding Fathers, whose rebellion against the English was, he believes, based on similarly noble motives.

'The danger can be . . .' (p. 77)

The danger can be that the road is really narrow. Not everyone can walk it, and if you don't live up to biblical standards, you risk being left behind, alone and alienated. It's hard enough being a teenager without having to make the path so difficult with no room for mistakes. God knows I made plenty.

Brian Dannelly, Director and co-writer of *Saved!*

(MGM pictures, 2004)

Source

www.savedmovie.com

Background

Saved! is set in an American Christian high school. Mary is a born-again Christian, and all is going well for her until she discovers that her boyfriend Dean is gay. In order to 'cure' him, Mary sleeps with Dean (she mistakenly thought that she had received a vision telling her to do so) and gets pregnant. Instead of supporting her, her Christian friends abandon her and she starts to hang out with the two non-believing misfits in her school. She has a crisis of faith, questioning whether God really exists.

'It is different . . .' (p. 89)

It is different, yeah, it's a different morality. Get used to it or go home.

The Doctor in *Doctor Who*

Source

Doctor Who, episode 3 – 'The Unquiet Dead', BBC TV

Background

Doctor Who was first broadcast by BBC television in 1963, and remained a staple of the BBC schedules until 1989, making it the longest running sci-fi television show in the world. To the delight of the show's committed fanbase, it was revamped and returned for a new series in 2005. This quote comes from the third episode ('The Unquiet Dead') of the new series, which was first broadcast on Saturday 9 April 2005.

The Doctor is a Time Lord from the planet Gallifrey. He travels in space and time, opposing evil and generally saving the day. He is over 900 years old and has two hearts. From time to time, when his body gets worn out (or when an actor gets fed up of playing the role) the Doctor regenerates. Christopher Ecclestone – the Doctor quoted here – is the ninth official Doctor, following in the footsteps of William Hartnell, Patrick Troughton, Jon Pertwee, Tom Baker, Peter Davison, Colin Baker, Sylvester McCoy and Paul McGann (who played the Doctor in a single TV-movie made for the American market). Peter Cushing also played the role in two films in the 1960s, but his Doctor is not considered to be part of the official canon. After the broadcast of the first episode of the new series, Ecclestone announced that he did not intend to film a second series. Subsequently the BBC announced that David Tennant will be the tenth official Doctor.

The episode is set in Cardiff in 1869. An alien race called the Gelth have been deprived of their bodies as a consequence of the Time War, and are now trapped in a gaseous state. When the Doctor manages to contact the Gelth by means of a seance, they claim to be few in number and needing to make use of dead bodies that are no longer wanted (this story turns out to be false, but the Doctor is unaware of that when he says the lines quoted here). The Doctor's assistant Rose (Billie Piper) argues that it's wrong to let the Gelth use dead bodies like this, but the Doctor likens their plan to organ donors, and tells Rose that her unreasonable sensibilities in the matter could result in a whole race of people dying out.

'I only draw the line . . .' (p. 101)

> I only draw the line of what's unacceptable according to my personal taste, not by what other people judge as acceptable. I do things that suit me and feel right.
>
> Marilyn Manson

Source

Interviewed in *Q* magazine, April 2004

Background

Marilyn Manson is a controversial goth-metal solo artist who has probably never released an album that didn't require an 'explicit content' warning sticker.

Manson went on to list some of the things that, right now, he would not do: 'grow a beard or play an acoustic guitar. Wear jeans onstage, have a bath . . . those things to me are pretty twisted'. Beware of the possibility of image-perpetuating tongue in cheek here.

For Further Reading

D. A. Carson, *The Gagging of God: Christianity Confronts Pluralism* (Apollos, 1996)

Colin Chapman, *Cross and Crescent: Responding to the Challenge of Islam* (IVP, 1996)

Dennis McCallum, *The Death of Truth: Responding to multiculturalism, the rejection of reason and the new postmodern diversity* (Bethany House Publishers, 1996)

Alister E. McGrath, *A Passion for Truth: The intellectual coherence of evangelicalism* (Apollos, 1996)

Harold A. Netland, *Dissonant Voices: Religious pluralism and the question of truth* (Apollos, 1991)

Harold A. Netland, *Encountering Religious Pluralism: The Challenge to Christian Faith & Mission* (Apollos, 2002)

Lesslie Newbigin, *The Gospel in a Pluralist Society* (SPCK, 1991)

Vinoth Ramachandra, *Faiths in Conflict? Christian integrity in a multicultural world* (IVP, 1999)

Chris Wright, *Thinking Clearly About the Uniqueness of Jesus* (Monarch, 1997)

Other Titles in the Talking About Series

Sex and the Cynics: Talking About the Search for Love

Playing God: Talking About Ethics in Medicine and Technology (due for publication Spring 2006)

Spooked: Talking About the Supernatural (due for publication Spring 2006)

Other Titles from Damaris Books

Get More Like Jesus While Watching TV
by Nick Pollard and Steve Couch

If Only by Nick Pollard

Back In Time: A Thinking Fan's Guide to Doctor Who
by Peter S. Williams, Tony Watkins and Steve Couch
(due for publication Autumn 2005)

Dark Matter: A Thinking Fan's Guide to Philip Pullman
by Tony Watkins

Matrix Revelations: A Thinking Fan's Guide to the Matrix Trilogy
edited by Steve Couch

I Wish I Could Believe In Meaning
by Peter S. Williams

Teenagers: Why Do They Do That?
by Nick Pollard

Join Damaris and receive

Discounts on other products from Damaris Books and Damaris Publishing.

Access to Web pages containing up-to-date information about popular culture.

To find out about *free membership* of Damaris go to www.damaris.org

DAMARIS
www.damaris.org

DAMARIS
www.DamarisBooks.com

"Relating Christian faith and contemporary culture"

CultureWatch
(free access website)

CultureWatch explores the message behind the media through hundreds of articles and study guides on films, books, music and television. It is written from a distinctively Christian angle, but is appropriate for people of all faiths and people of no faith at all.

CULTUREWATCH
http://www.damaris.org/cw

Tools for Talks

(subscription website)

A one-stop preparation shop for Christian speakers and Bible teachers, enabling you to teach the message of the Bible in the language of contemporary popular culture.

Hundreds of quotes and illustrations from the latest films, music and TV with new material added weekly

All this, plus the complete text of the IVP New Bible Commentary and the Index for Hodder and Stoughton's Thematic Study Bible.

tools for Talks
www.toolsfortalks.com

DAMARIS
www.DamarisBooks.com

The Quest
(CD ROM)

Your journey into the heart of spirituality.

Take your own route, take your own time, seek your own answers to the big philosophical and religious questions with this self-updating oracle for your PC.

The Quest grows as you search, with free updates automatically downloaded from the web.

THE QUEST
www.questforanswers.com